SPEAKING ILL OF THE DEAD:

Jerks in Florida History

SPEAKING ILL OF THE DEAD:

Jerks in Florida History

E. Lynne Wright

Guilford, Connecticut

To buy books in quantity for corporate use
or incentives, call **(800) 962-0973**
or e-mail **premiums@GlobePequot.com.**

Text design: Sheryl P. Kober
Project editor: Lauren Szalkiewicz
Layout artist: Sue Murray

Library of Congress Cataloging-in-Publication Data

Wright, E. Lynne, 1931-
 Speaking ill of the dead : jerks in Florida history / E. Lynne Wright.
    pages cm
 Includes bibliographical references and index.
 ISBN 978-0-7627-7854-6
1. Florida—History—Anecdotes. 2. Florida—Biography—Anecdotes. 3.
Outlaws—Florida—Biography—Anecdotes. 4. Rogues and
vagabonds—Florida—Biography—Anecdotes. 5.
Criminals—Illinois—Chicago—Biography—Anecdotes. I. Title. II.
Title: Jerks in Florida history.
 F311.6.W77 2013
 975.9—dc23

                                                        2013018901

Printed in the United States of America

10 9 8 7 6 5 4 3 2 1

Contents

CONTENTS

Acknowledgments

Sincere thanks to historian Alvin Lederer for taking the time for that long, informative telephone conversation with me, a stranger seeking information about Edgar Watson. Thanks, too, to Dawn Hugh and the staff at HistoryMiami for all their help with information and photos. I also want to send thanks to the Historical Society of Palm Beach County, Gwyn Surface at the *Palm Beach Post,* and Dozier School survivor Roger Kiser Sr. As always, my dealings with N. Adam Watson and the staff at the State Archives of Florida in Tallahassee were such a pleasure, I can't thank them enough.

I'm sure no editors have ever been more patient, helpful, or wise than Erin Turner and Courtney Oppel. I will be forever grateful to them. Finally, I thank my computer/Internet expert, Dr. George Wright. I couldn't have done it without him.

Introduction

When I was approached to write a book about speaking ill of the dead and jerks in Florida history, I thought it sounded like fun. After all, how many opportunities do we get to break rules we've heard ever since we were children? *"We don't say bad things about the dead."* And as for there being jerks in Florida history—well, let's just say that any time I mentioned the title of the book I was working on to writer friends, most of them covered their mouths with one hand, attempting to hide the smirks they couldn't quite suppress. I knew what they were thinking: "Jerks—in Florida history? Surely you jest!" A few of the kinder ones would hastily add that since our beautiful state has always attracted people from all over the world, it is therefore logical that we might have more than our share of jerks in our history too.

But as expected, there were usually a few who muttered something about not all of the jerks being dead and, "Elections, elections, elections." Our recent history concerning the electoral process can be rather dismaying to those of us who cling to the idea that each person's vote is sacred. Then the living jerks are out in force, following paths laid out for them by jerks long dead. Votes are and always have been sacred for some among us—that is, unless you belong to the wrong political party, or your skin is the wrong color, or you speak with an accent, or . . . well, you get the idea.

Then, too, times have changed, and some things that were considered acceptable early in our history are frowned upon now. Dr. Weedon's actions following the death of his famous Seminole patient, Osceola, would fall into that category. I shudder to think what would happen today to any doctor who might undertake behavior similar to Dr. Weedon's, and yet at the time it didn't seem to occur to him or to others that even a highly respected physician may not engage in behavior disrespectful to a human body.

The aftermath of war, especially for those on the losing side, could conceivably inspire some very jerk-like conduct among survivors. This is what happened when, under the influence of that charismatic actor John Wilkes Booth, a very young Lewis Powell, aka Payne, turned into the worst sort of jerk who eventually paid for his actions with his life.

It may seem a bit of a stretch to include a plant in a discussion of jerks, but if ever an organism belonging to the kingdom of greenery could be labeled as such, the water hyacinth certainly fills the bill. The plant has been the cause of serious damage to docks, bridges, and crops and has indirectly brought about death to animals, snakes, and fish. To estimate the cost of the damage caused by this beautiful plant is impossible, and the expense will be ongoing, with no prospects of it ever ending.

An undeniable truth accepted by most people is that greed is at the bottom of countless acts of despicable behavior. It always was and most likely always will be so. Greed inspires even some of the nicest people to exhibit nasty behavior. The lure of making a lot of money in a big hurry with little effort appeals to many people in all walks of life. This temptation is illustrated in the chapter about Ben Hecht, the famous Hollywood writer who couldn't ever have enough, and in the tale of the friend of Marjorie Kinnan Rawlings who couldn't resist the chance for some easy money, no matter that it would cause much pain to someone who considered her a friend.

It would be impossible to discuss jerks in the history of any area of our country south of the Mason-Dixon line without focusing more than once on racism. Unfortunately, Florida shares that dubious distinction. Anyone who doubts this ugly truth needs to be made aware of the countless numbers of law enforcement officers, judges, lawyers, politicians, legislators, and even governors who have embraced racist policies over the years, sometimes openly, at other times in secret. The grim details of this important part of our history won't make anyone feel good, but they must be remembered and told. The tales of individual violence are repugnant in themselves, but the history of an entire organization devoted to waging war against a progressive society in which all men and women are created equal makes for uncomfortable but essential reading.

A sad fact of life, but one that cannot be ignored, is that even heroes can be jerks at times. Some things hurt, but to watch someone we have crowned with the mantle of hero fall before our eyes can be devastating. It is very difficult to ignore the pain and tell ourselves the hero is human, humans make mistakes, or the hero didn't really mean to do that. The story of the Mercury Thirteen is one of those tales. It makes us want to find an excuse for non-heroic actions, but even the old standby, "Times were different then," doesn't always work. Mean-spirited, selfish, sexist, arrogant, and egotistical behaviors are still mean-spirited, selfish, sexist, arrogant, and egotistical, no matter who is exhibiting those traits, what gender they are, or where they are strutting their stuff. It just hurts more when our heroes, both male and female, flaunt their unfortunate attitudes so openly and seemingly without regard for anyone's feelings.

Some of these stories are cringe-inducing, such as the unspeakable actions of the men who were entrusted with overseeing the lives of troubled boys in the Dozier School and the beast who murdered little Adam Walsh. As I researched these crimes, I felt ashamed to belong to the same human race as the perpetrators. Yet, in the case of Adam Walsh, though we fervently wish it had never happened, some good came of it, thanks to his grieving parents' ceaseless work to help establish new laws to prevent such a thing from ever happening to another child. And though it is painful to admit it, those stories and other revolting ones, too, are part of our history. How we wish they had never happened. But they did happen and they happened here in the Sunshine State, whether or not we care to be reminded of it.

The majority of the jerks among these chapters knew exactly what they were doing when they were doing it. They planned their actions meticulously and are 100 percent responsible for their deeds and for the consequences. We must never totally forget what dark or repugnant actions some of us are capable of carrying out, and above all, we must never let down our guard where our children are concerned.

CHAPTER 1

Dr. Weedon's Gruesome Surgery

It was a remarkable friendship that developed between Osceola, the famed Seminole leader who had been shamefully captured by the Americans under a flag of truce, and Frederick Weedon, the physician who cared for Osceola during his captivity but was a member of the same military that had committed an atrocious act of treachery against him.

Osceola passionately dedicated his life to the cause of resistance to Indian removal from their native lands and their relocation to unknown western territories. With the threshold of his life cut short by the dishonorable violation of the rules of warfare, Osceola's fame continued to increase, spreading even among the whites who belonged on the side of those responsible for his capture and eventually his death.

The forces who captured Osceola have mostly been forgotten, but the name of the Seminole warrior they seized is even now spread across the United States, naming twenty towns, three counties, one borough, two townships, a state park, a national forest, two lakes, and one dormitory hall at Florida State University.

Although Osceola was believed to be the son of an Indian woman and a white trader father, in some eyes he could still legitimately claim, as he sometimes did with great fervor, that he was "a pure-blood Muskogee." His assertion was considered valid because Muskogee was the name often given to the Lower Creeks, and since the Seminole and Creek Indians are matrilineal societies, their men are always looked upon as members of their mother's clan.

Osceola was a boy when his family was forced to flee Andrew Jackson's forces during the First Seminole War, but in ensuing years, he would observe the white man's brutalities, broken words, and violated treaties. He honestly yearned to live peacefully with

Portrait of Dr. Frederick R. Weedon, St. Augustine, Florida

the white invaders, yet remained proud of his Indian blood and refused to dishonor it.

Shortly after the First Seminole War ended in 1818, Spain sold Florida to the United States government, causing countless Seminoles to face uncertain futures and the prospect of starvation. There seemed to be few alternatives open to them, so in 1823, by signing the Treaty of Moultrie Creek, the Seminoles agreed to accept confinement on a four-million-acre reservation in return for being provided with at least twenty years of financial support from the United States government. However, as time passed, white settlers encroached on those desirable Indian lands, skirmishes increased, and Indian chiefs were tricked into signing deceptive treaties.

By 1830, as the result of unrelenting white demands, Congress passed the Indian Removal Act, a blatant violation of the Moultrie Treaty. A few years later, this was followed by Indians being duped into signing bogus treaties at Payne's Landing and Fort Gibson that would require them to move west into what was then Arkansas Territory. When Indian agent Wiley Thompson attempted to have the most prominent of the Indian chiefs sign their consent to emigrate, they refused, insisting that the Moultrie Treaty still had nine years to run. Thompson's fury was matched by that of the young Osceola, who was not a chief but was fast becoming a respected leader. With his knife, Osceola angrily stabbed the treaty papers where they lay on the table, loudly declaring for all to hear that it would be the only way he would sign it.

It was the beginning of bad feelings between the Indian agent and the charismatic Osceola. The bitterness escalated until a few months later when, according to Thompson, Osceola came to his office in a foul mood, insulting him and hurling nasty language at the agent. It was not the first time Osceola exhibited such behavior, but this time Thompson, fed up with the insults, ordered his men to handcuff Osceola and confine him in jail for several days. Chastened after a time, Osceola apologized to Thompson and not only was he freed, but in an apparent gesture to get on his good side and show there were no hard feelings, Thompson presented the young Indian with an expensive, custom-made rifle. The generous move would later prove to be a profound mistake on Thompson's part.

Although two subordinate Seminole chiefs, Holata and Charlie Emathla, agreed to the removal of their people to the west, the more powerful chiefs did not. Enraged by what he considered deception of the Seminole people on the part of the two Seminole leaders who agreed, Osceola waylaid them when they were returning to their village. Holata somehow managed to escape, but in a rage, Osceola shot and killed Emathla. He then took the silver and gold coins wrapped in a kerchief that Emathla had with him, which he had been paid upon signing the removal agreement. Before he left, Osceola scattered the coins on the ground, furiously shouting, "This is made of red man's blood!" No one dared to disobey his order that the body not be touched, and Emathla's body and his coins reportedly remained on the ground undisturbed for two years before his bones were finally buried by white soldiers.

However, Osceola was not finished. In December 1835, as the Second Seminole War was beginning, the firebrand warrior spied Wiley Thompson and another officer enjoying a stroll outside Fort King. Using the excellent rifle Thompson had presented to him, Osceola took aim, shot, and killed both men.

As his reputation grew among his own people and, begrudgingly, even among white Americans, so too did the US Army's determination to capture Osceola despite the growing admiration for his skills and courage. At the same time, a succession of Army commanders, eight in all, took turns being the subjects of increasing pressure to demonstrate some sign of success in the task of Indian removal to the west—all eight of them failed.

In 1837, General Thomas Jesup, the new commander, arranged a meeting with Osceola and his group under a flag of truce. When they were seated, the Indians became increasingly aware that they were being silently surrounded by white troops. Then, without any discussion, under orders from General Jesup, the Seminoles were seized and imprisoned at Fort Marion in St. Augustine, known today as the Castillo de San Marcos.

Word of Osceola's capture initiated celebrations as it spread throughout the country, but those cheers turned to outrage—even among white settlers—when the dishonor of it became known. Some whites were convinced that the action would prolong the war by feeding the fury of the Seminoles, inspiring them to fight even harder. Furthermore, although he didn't know it then, General Jesup would spend the rest of his life attempting to justify his outrageous order.

Because previously some twenty prisoners had escaped from Fort Marion, the decision was made to send Osceola and other Seminole prisoners on a steamer, the *Poinsett,* to the more secure Fort Moultrie in South Carolina. Dr. Frederick Weedon had been caring for Osceola during his capture, and at his Indian patient's request, the doctor agreed to accompany him on the trip.

Dr. Weedon was a highly respected physician in the Baltimore area. He had returned there, his hometown, after studying medicine in Philadelphia. Following the family tradition, he then joined the military, received his commission as a captain in the cavalry in 1808, and entered the service in 1813.

Weedon married a wealthy Baltimore girl, Mary Marable, and they made a home in Alabama near the Florida border, but Mary died in 1816. The doctor took another wife, Mary W. Thompson, who was also wealthy. The Weedons lived for a time in Alabama before moving to Tallahassee for five years. After that, they crossed two hundred miles of Florida Territory with their eight children to settle in St. Augustine.

While he practiced medicine and reported to his military group periodically, Dr. Weedon also purchased and worked a large citrus grove. He accepted an appointment as justice of the peace in August 1835, and to fill up his spare time, in 1836 the busy doctor took on the duties as St. Augustine's mayor.

Even after officially separating from the military, Dr. Weedon maintained his connections with them, which resulted in his agreeing to oversee the prisoners in Fort Marion at St. Augustine. That was how he became acquainted with Osceola, whose health was beginning to cause him problems. Consequently, when the army decided to move Osceola and the 202 other Indians to Fort Moultrie on Sullivan's Island in Charleston Harbor, the Seminoles, who had come to trust Weedon, pressed the doctor to accompany them. He consented to the move and to work for a salary of $150 per month.

For some time, a rumor had been circulating that Dr. Weedon had some ulterior motive when he agreed to attend Osceola. There was talk that it might have something to do with the fact that his second wife, Mary Thompson Weedon, was the sister of Wiley Thompson, the Indian agent shot and killed by Osceola. Then, too, several acquaintances of the doctor's believed he planned to write a book about Osceola, but none of this has been proven.

Their cordial relationship, however, was authentic. The two men unexpectedly developed a friendship that grew as the doctor spent time providing care for his patient's occasional fevers. The fevers apparently were the result of malaria, but prisoners also suffered from bites from fleas and possibly from lice in the less-than-pristine surroundings of the prison. It was also possible that Osceola suffered from strep throat, or quinsy as it was called at the time, with accompanying inflammation and abscesses. All these conditions were much more serious in those days because antibiotics did not yet exist.

That the prisoners were held on a secure island resulted in their being able to enjoy more freedoms and more visitors than they would have had otherwise. Among Osceola's visitors were his two wives, several children, and occasional artists who wanted to paint pictures of the famous prisoner in his colorful regalia. The prisoner was agreeable, seeming to enjoy his fame when he wasn't feeling too poorly from his health issues. He particularly savored the conversation while his portrait was being painted by the renowned artist George Catlin, one of whose paintings of Osceola became very well known.

For a time, Osceola accepted the ministrations of the white doctor, even bestowing a few artifacts on him to show his gratitude. The gifts included a sort of short rifle called a carbine; a lock of Osceola's hair; a small brass pipe; a silver concho, which was an ornament that was sewn to the end of a sash; two silver earrings; a man's woolen garter, such as was usually worn by men to secure their leggings; and a sheath knife with a carved ivory grip.

However, as he became more ill and his breathing became more labored, Osceola depended more and more on the prayers and ministrations of the Indian medicine men who had been summoned. Dr. Weedon even called in Dr. Benjamin Strobel, another physician from the Medical College of Charleston, to confer, but although both men believed they could have saved the patient's life had they been permitted to treat him, Osceola refused their further treatments.

Clearly, the Seminole chief knew he was near death. According to a quote from Dr. Weedon's diary—which was preserved and has been shared by his great-granddaughter, Mary McNeer Ward— Osceola asked "that his Bones Should be permitted to remain in peace and that I should take them To Florida & place them where I Knew they would not be disturbed."

At six the next morning, January 30, 1838, he asked for his "full dress," which consisted of the clothes he wore "in time of war," including three ostrich plumes and silver spurs. After donning them, he painted half of his face, neck, and hands red, a custom that traditionally accompanied the oath of war. He then shook hands with all who were present, white and Indian, wives and children. He grasped his scalping knife in one hand, and with assistance lowered himself to his bed. By 6:20 a.m., with a slight smile on his face, Osceola was dead.

While the other Seminoles mourned their chief, the two physicians, Weedon and Strobel, used the few hours while a coffin was being constructed to make a cast of Osceola's head, shoulders, and upper torso. Although the other Seminoles disapproved of this practice and found it upsetting, the doctors were complying with orders given by Captain Pitcairn Morrison, the officer in charge of the prisoners.

Captain Morrison also blatantly disregarded another Seminole tradition. Their accepted custom required that most of a dead Seminole's possessions were to be buried with him, but Captain Morrison ordered that this tradition also be ignored, so Osceola was not buried with his.

But neither of these insults could compare to what else was done to the body after it was placed in the coffin.

It is uncertain just when he was alone long enough with Osceola's body to perform the gruesome act, but there was an interval during which Dr. Weedon had the audacity to deliberately and skillfully separate Osceola's head from his body. After draining as much fluid from the head as possible, he replaced the head in the coffin, took the handkerchiefs that the Indian always wore around his neck, and rewrapped them in the same way to hide the incision. He then closed the coffin.

Sometime shortly before the funeral, the doctor removed the head from the corpse and closed the coffin once more.

Why would a respected man of science do such a ghoulish thing? To say that he wanted to preserve a specimen for the benefit of science hardly excuses him for ignoring the Indians' feelings and their honored traditions.

At some point after the funeral, Dr. Weedon wrote several narratives about Osceola's funeral. None of them ever mentioned that his possessions were not buried with his body according to the Seminole tradition. Even more importantly, Weedon also omitted the fact that Osceola's head was not in his coffin either. But that was not the end of the insults heaped upon the departed spirit.

Although Osceola had made clear his wishes "that his Bones Should be permitted to remain in peace" in Florida, his wish was not honored. His body was buried on the US Army post in Fort Moultrie, South Carolina, adding to the dishonor of his missing head and the removed artifacts.

According to Weedon's great-granddaughter, May McNeer Ward, Dr. Weedon preserved Osceola's head, most likely with alcohol, to facilitate taking it with him when he completed his military assignment and returned to his home and office in St. Augustine. His actions seem grotesque and inappropriate today, unquestionably qualifying him as a bona fide jerk in the twenty-first century. But at that time, it was an accepted practice for doctors and medical museums to preserve the heads of those they considered savages, which resulted in large collections of them in some medical institutions.

According to his family members, Dr. Weedon went one very large step further with his unconventional conduct, in that he would hang Osceola's head overnight on the bedposts of his young sons as punishment for their misbehavior. It was convenient for him, since both his office and his adjoining drug store—where he sometimes displayed the head—were attached to his home.

After a few years, Weedon gave Osceola's head to Daniel Whitehurst, who was married to the eldest Weedon daughter, Henrietta. Whitehurst owned and published the *St. Augustine News* and was also a lawyer before he went on to study medicine under Dr. Valentine Mott, the most distinguished surgeon in the country at the time and a founder of New York University Medical School. With Dr. Weedon's approval, his son-in-law turned Osceola's head over to Dr. Mott.

Mott gratefully accepted the donation and eventually included it in the collection of heads in his museum of pathological specimens. In the letter of acceptance he wrote to Dr. Whitehurst upon receiving the head, he stated his intentions to keep it in his home library, since he feared it might be stolen were he to place it in the museum at the university.

But in 1858, the New York Academy of Medicine published the catalogue of the Surgical and Pathological Museum of Valentine Mott, M.D., L.L.D., Emeritus Professor of Surgery in the University of the City of New York, listing: "Miscellaneous—No. 1132 Head of Osceola, the great Seminole chief (undoubted). Presented by Dr. Whitehurst of St. Augustine."

However, the museum caught fire in 1866, destroying many of its specimens. That the head of the most famous Seminole warrior was lost in the fire has never been proven, but the head has never been recovered. Most non-Indian authorities believe the head was lost in the fire. Nevertheless, many Seminoles believe the head still exists and hope that someday they will be able to reunite it with the body of the great warrior who shared their love of Florida and died to keep his people in their beloved homeland.

Dr. Weedon decided to take advantage of the opportunity to enlarge his land holdings when the Armed Occupation Act was passed in 1842. To encourage settlers to clear and populate vast areas of land in Florida, the government granted tracts of land to whites who would brave the unsettled frontier, never mind any Indian rights. Dr. Weedon accepted the offer and moved onto 160 acres in Fort Pierce, but when fire destroyed much of the emerging settlement, the aging doctor returned to St. Augustine.

His wife died in 1849, leaving her husband alone and in failing health. Weedon then moved to Key West to be with his daughter Henrietta and her husband, Dr. Whitehurst, who had been acting as the surgeon for Fort Jefferson in the Dry Tortugas. Weedon died there in 1857.

Since 1930, when the Florida Historical Society first requested the return of Osceola's bones to his homeland, the states of Florida and South Carolina have engaged in an ongoing intermittent competition for possession of the remains. Fort Moultrie, where Osceola was buried, is part of the US Department of Interior, National Park Service. Floridians point out that as recently as 1966, park guards discovered evidence of digging at the gravesite. Thus, Floridians are convinced South Carolinians are incapable of properly caring for the grave, while Carolinians are certain Florida would just turn the grave into another one of their gaudy tourist attractions.

Meanwhile, the Seminoles patiently wait for their great warrior to return to his home.

CHAPTER 2

John Wilkes Booth's Florida Conspirator

He was the youngest son in a family of nine. His father, George Cader Powell, was a Baptist minister. As a child, he brought home so many injured animals to care for, his sisters, who adored him, nicknamed him "Doc." But at the age of twenty-one, he died on a scaffold with three other conspirators after having slashed the United States secretary of state where he lay in his sick bed, then shot at, knifed, and mercilessly beat three other people, in an attempt to fulfill his part of a plan to exterminate the United States president, the vice president, the secretary of state, and General Ulysses S. Grant. How did Lewis Powell, the handsome young man who often expressed a desire to become a minister, instead turn into a jerk who participated in one of the ugliest conspiracies in this nation's history?

The Powell family, originally from Georgia, had moved for a time to Alabama before finally settling just over the border in Hamilton County, Florida. Lewis was four years old when they moved on to Live Oak in Suwannee County, Florida, at a time when rumblings about abolition and states' rights were beginning to grow louder.

To supplement the family income while he worked as a rural clergyman, George Powell worked the family farm and practiced as a blacksmith, and occasionally filled in as schoolmaster at a local backwoods school. His wife, Patience Caroline, uncommonly well educated for a female in those times, assumed the responsibility for the education of their nine children.

Lewis enjoyed learning and was so devoted to his Sunday school lessons and prayer meetings that he taught religion classes when he was a young teen. Still, he loved being outdoors, and

Lewis Thornton Powell

could be heard singing hymns as he fished, did his chores, and played with his various pets. Once, as he played with one of his favorites, a mule that was as much a pet as a dog would be to most boys, Lewis received a kick from his mule that fractured his jaw and knocked out a molar. Despite his concerned mother's wishes, Lewis's father prevailed, and the boy was allowed to keep the mule he loved so dearly.

He was growing strong and handsome and measured a bit over six feet at seventeen years. While the whole country seemed to be rumbling with talk of states' rights, abolition, and secession, many young men developed a feverish interest in the military, even in secluded Live Oak. Lewis was no exception. In 1861, on his seventeenth birthday, though he gave his age as nineteen, he and a friend enlisted in the Jasper Blues of Hamilton County. His parents reluctantly accepted his decision, and he slowly adjusted to military life.

His regiment became Company I, Second Florida Infantry, when it moved to the Jacksonville area, then on to Richmond, Virginia, just as the heartening news spread of the first Confederate victory at Manassas. Powell's group spent the next two months guarding the Manassas prisoners near Richmond. It is believed that was where Powell first met John Wilkes Booth when they were supposedly introduced backstage after a performance. The intellectual actor with a slender frame and resonant voice and the big, rough soldier with a small, thin voice seemed to find something appealing in each other. They met again several times in Richmond before Powell's division moved on to Yorktown.

In Yorktown, Powell saw action for the first time, soon followed by fighting at Williamsburg, Seven Pines, Gaines Mill, Frayser's Farm, and Second Manassas. By then, his one-year enlistment was up, but he reenlisted for another year, eager to collect his fifty-dollar bonus.

He was becoming battle-hardened in campaigns at Yorktown, Antietam, Fredericksburg, and Chancellorsville, among others, but was deeply saddened when he learned of the combat death of

Oliver, one of his older brothers. His sadness increased when his other brother, George, was wounded.

Powell's unit moved into Pennsylvania to join other troops in the fierce battle at Gettysburg, where he was wounded in his right wrist and taken prisoner. Since it was not an incapacitating injury, he was put to work as a prisoner/nurse. Lewis had grown up and fit into his job easily, even being addressed as and answering to "Doctor Powell." He also enjoyed spending time with an attractive female volunteer nurse, Margaret Branson. Quietly pro-Confederate, Margaret most likely provided Powell with a blue uniform that would aid him in an escape attempt.

Details of his escape are obscure, but he did escape, slipping through Union lines into Virginia. Then, wearing a gray uniform he somehow procured, he was making a fruitless search for his old unit when he came across members of Colonel Mosbey's Virginia cavalry and decided to join them instead.

An unusual unit, Mosbey's Rangers, as they were known, lived civilian lives until they were needed to make a raid. When the raid ended, they returned to their nonmilitary lives. During the year Powell spent with the Rangers, he boarded with relatives of General W. H. Payne, whose surname he adopted when he deserted the Rangers on January 1, 1865. He donned civilian clothes, used his adopted name, Lewis Paine (sometimes spelled Payne), to sign a pledge of allegiance to the United States government, then sold his horse and headed for Baltimore.

Powell used many aliases in his short life, but he became most familiar as Lewis Paine.

Upon reaching Baltimore, he renewed his friendship with Margaret Branson and her sister when he took a room in their mother's boardinghouse. For a time, Paine lived off the money he received from selling his horse, but it has been suggested, although not proven, that in addition, he received funds from the Confederate secret service. However he managed his finances, he spent much time reading, mainly medical texts, and escorting the Branson sisters on long walks.

It was on one of his walks past Barnum's Hotel that he met and renewed his acquaintance with the slender actor standing on the hotel steps, John Wilkes Booth, ardent secessionist, favorite actor of Southern audiences, and agent to the Confederate secret service.

Certainly, when Booth recognized the big, battle-hardened youth, he must have instantly realized what a valuable ally Paine would be in the plan the actor had been formulating, a plan he estimated would call for help from six other men. Booth's scheme was to abduct President Lincoln and members of his cabinet, haul them across the Potomac River into the South, and so force the North to pay ransom and agree to the South's demands for a peace agreement.

Gathering at a Baltimore boardinghouse run by Mrs. Mary Surratt, Paine met the rest of the group Booth had rounded up to work out details for the kidnapping. They included Mrs. Surratt and her twenty-year-old son, John, a courier for the Confederate secret service who knew all the less-known routes through Maryland; Samuel Arnold, a thirty-one-year-old school chum of Booth's whose family owned a well-known Baltimore bakery and who knew parts of the city few others did; and Michael O'Laughlen, another longtime friend whose family lived across the street from Booth's, who was out of the army, with nothing to do and looking for excitement. Then there was twenty-two-year-old pharmacist's assistant and avid hunter David Herold, whose knowledge of the area, including the backwoods through which they would have to travel, would be vital. Last was George Atzerodt, originally from Prussia, whose knowledge of boats and familiarity with local waters was essential for the group's escape. And, of course, there was fiercely loyal, big, very strong Lewis Paine.

The plan called for the men to rush the carriage conveying Lincoln, who was supposedly on his way to see a play, and then carry him to a boat that would ferry him across the Potomac to Virginia. The simple plan failed completely when they discovered Lincoln was not in the carriage.

Enraged but undeterred, Booth wasted no time investigating where their failures had been. He immediately formed a new plan, and decided this one would not spare the president's life.

Things were going badly for the Confederate states at this time. On April 3, Richmond fell to the Union. On April 9, General Robert E. Lee surrendered to General Ulysses S. Grant at Appomattox. The mood of the South was grim. Drastic action needed to be taken if the direction of the war was to be turned around. Kidnapping was out. Not only was he convinced it was necessary to assassinate President Lincoln, but Booth decided they would also take out the vice president, the secretary of state, and General Grant.

By April 14, Booth's select group had dwindled. Arnold and O'Laughlen had second thoughts and backed out. John Surratt was on his way to Canada, carrying messages to the Confederate secretary of state, who happened to be in Montreal. But Booth's plan was in place, and he was convinced he had all the men he needed to carry it out.

Booth learned Lincoln would be present at a play at Ford's Theatre that night. Since Booth was quite familiar with every part of the theater building, he was the logical one to attend to the president. Through his sources, he learned that General Grant had left town, so that was one less target to focus on. Atzerodt's job was to assassinate Vice President Johnson where he stayed at the Kirkwood House. Paine would take out Secretary of State William H. Seward at his mansion near the White House, known to the locals as the "Clubhouse" because it had previously been used as an exclusive gathering place for members of Congress. Now, though, it was the Seward home, and it was where the secretary was recovering from a concussion, fractured jaw, and arm, the result of a carriage accident. Herold was to accompany Paine to and from Seward's home, because Paine was unfamiliar with Washington streets and Herold knew them well. Booth armed his fellow conspirators with guns and knives, and all agreed to attack at exactly 10:00 p.m.

Unbeknownst to Booth, at 10:00 p.m., Atzerodt was trying to find the courage to carry out his assignment—at the Kirkwood House bar. He never did find it; indeed, after some time and more than a few drinks, he left the hotel, mounted his horse, and rode away into the night.

While Herold attended to their horses in the shadows nearby, Paine knocked on the door of the darkened Seward home at precisely 10:00 p.m. carrying a small box carefully wrapped by Herold, the pharmacist's assistant. He informed William Bell, the servant who answered, that he had a package of medicine for the secretary. Bell politely informed Paine that Mr. Seward wasn't to be disturbed, but he would see that Seward got the medicine. They bickered for a few moments, and then Paine roughly pushed past the young black servant and started up the stairs. Responding to the disturbance, Frederick Seward, who was the son of the secretary and was also assistant secretary of state, met Paine at the top of the stairs, insisting his father was not to be disturbed. Paine turned and appeared to be starting back down the stairs, when he suddenly whirled around with a revolver in his hand, aimed at Frederick's head. It misfired, but Paine proceeded to club his target's head so forcefully that the pistol broke, fracturing young Seward's skull as it did.

Seward's daughter, Fanny, had been sitting in the sickroom in semidarkness, watching over her father along with a soldier nurse, Sergeant Robinson. Responding to the disturbance outside the closed bedroom, she opened the door and Paine shoved his way into the room. He pushed Fanny aside, lunged at Robinson, slashed him hard across the forehead, and sent him hurtling across the room. Confused by the commotion, the elderly, very ill patient lying in the bed rolled sideways as the assassin lunged for him. With all the strength in his powerful body, Paine plunged his knife, but fortunately missed the patient and gouged the sheets and mattress. He raised his arm again, missed again, and in the darkness, missed a third time before he finally connected with the elder Seward's flesh, and then manage to slice open the secretary's cheek and across his neck just as the old man was rolling sideways from his bed onto the floor.

By this time, Robinson recovered enough that he was able to grab Paine from behind. As they struggled, Paine stabbed over his shoulder, wounding the other man twice.

Fanny's screams reached her other brother, Gus, who was sleeping in another room. The bedlam jolted Gus awake and, still in his nightshirt, he rushed in to join the bloody struggle. Paine slashed his forehead too, muttering, "I'm mad! I'm mad!" then escaped from the room and bolted down the stairs.

Part of the way down, he encountered another man, Emerick Hansell, a State Department employee who had been assigned to the Seward home. Hensell fell to the floor as Paine gashed his back, the fifth victim.

David Herold, waiting outside in the shadows with his and Paine's horses, heard Fanny's screams from inside the house. When she opened the window and screamed, Herold hastily tied Paine's horse to a tree, jumped on his own horse, and galloped away.

Paine did finally escape from the house but, without his guide, had no idea which way to turn in the dark, totally unfamiliar area. Finally, after abandoning his horse, he hid in the woods for three long days until hunger and thirst drove him to seek the only place he could think of where he might be able to find food and water, the Surratt boardinghouse.

Suspecting the Surratt house might still be under surveillance, Paine tried to disguise himself by tearing a sleeve from his undershirt and knotting it to look like a cap. He put it on his head and picked up an axe, which in an uncanny stroke of luck he had found in the woods. He decided if the need arose, he would pretend to be a workman hired by Mrs. Surratt.

A group of officers from the War Department had come to the boardinghouse minutes before Paine did, arresting everyone inside. Unaware of the situation, Paine arrived, claiming he had been hired to dig a ditch for Mrs. Surratt. But when they brought her into the room and she denied knowing him, the officers immediately took him into custody with the others.

William Bell, the Seward servant, was interviewed a few days later and identified Paine as the attacker, sealing his fate. They immediately chained Paine's hands and feet and removed him to a ship, the *Saugus,* anchored alongside the *Montauk* in the Potomac River, where he joined Arnold, O'Laughlen, Atzerodt, a Ford's Theatre workman named Edman Spangler, and some other prisoners.

In the meantime, Herold, who felt bad about leaving Paine behind, nevertheless headed for a bridge to cross over to Maryland. He believed he would be safer there, as Maryland had not seceded but was predominately sympathetic to the Confederates.

In Maryland, quite by chance he ran into Booth, whose left leg had been badly injured when he had leaped from the Ford's Theatre box to the stage. Together, the two men made their way on horseback to the residence of Dr. Samuel Mudd, a Booth acquaintance and a Confederate supporter.

The doctor treated Booth's fractured leg and supplied him with crutches before the two men continued on their tortuous journey, day after day, all the way to Virginia, with occasional help from a few other Confederate sympathizers.

They had finally settled down for the night in a barn after having received the owner's permission. However, before long they heard soldiers outside and were dismayed to discover that the owner of the barn had quietly locked them inside. With the soldiers threatening to burn the barn down, Herold surrendered, leaving Booth to face the end alone. Still, he refused to give up even when the rapidly spreading flames engulfed him. He made a final effort to shoot his way out but was gunned down and had to be pulled from the inferno. Fatally wounded, Booth died in a few hours, insisting with his last breath that he died for his country.

His death did allow him to escape the misery of a trial his partners faced. At the direction of President Johnson, ten army officers formed a commission to try Samuel Arnold, George Atzerodt, David

Herold, Dr. Samuel Mudd, Michael O'Laughlen, Lewis Paine, Edward Spangler, and Mary Surratt.

Arnold, O'Laughlen, and Dr. Mudd were each sentenced to life in prison. Spangler, a carpenter and scene shifter at Ford's Theatre, was charged with aiding in Booth's escape and received a six-year sentence. Atzerodt, Herold, Paine, and Surratt were all sentenced to be hanged at 1:00 p.m. the following day, July 7, which incited a burst of activity.

The federal government had never executed a woman, but Mary Surratt's unquestionable guilt in the notorious case caused quite a stir. Then, too, a scaffold had to be built in a hurry, and with no mistakes. It must work perfectly. Also, families had to be notified.

Paine's father was sick in bed when the letter with its tragic news arrived in Live Oak the evening before the executions were scheduled. Nevertheless, Reverend Powell started to make the long trip but had only reached Jacksonville when he learned he was too late. His son was dead. His wife, having already lost one son in the war, was so devastated she would not begin to recover for two years.

During his brief incarceration, reports concerning Paine's attitude and behavior varied drastically. Some insisted he was an emotional ruin and had tried to kill himself by banging his head against the steel wall. He was said to be greatly upset over Mrs. Surratt's facing death, most likely reflecting his traditional chivalrous Southern upbringing. When his lawyer insisted doctors examine him to determine his sanity, they declared him sane. More than once, Paine expressed regret for his action, insisting over and over he had only wanted to help his country.

The public was not permitted to observe the execution, but reporters and military members gathered in large numbers to witness it. Mostly, curiosity was focused on Lewis Paine and Mary Surratt when the four prisoners, arms tied behind them, were brought to the yard to ascend the creaky wooden steps. Ministers recited prayers while the nooses were fixed in place around the prisoners' necks and white hoods dropped over their heads.

At 1:25 p.m., Captain Christian Rath, the assigned executioner, clapped his hands three times. The third clap signaled waiting Reserve Corps veterans to knock away the supporting timbers and when they did, four bodies plunged and jerked, necks broken, with the exception of Paine, who writhed and twisted for nearly five minutes, strangling horribly.

The bodies were immediately buried a short distance away in the prison yard, but were reburied more than once when the facilities were moved. Eventually, they were released to their families, all except for Lewis Paine. Since his family moved several times in Florida after the executions, it is possible they never received notification to claim his body.

In 1993, a government anthropologist who was working with Native American skulls from a collection from the Smithsonian Institution came across the skull of an unnamed white male. Within months, it was positively identified as the skull of Lewis Paine, confirmed by the healed fracture and missing molar in the left jaw. The rest of his remains were never found. Some might believe it a fitting end for the jerk who was John Wilkes Booth's Florida coconspirator.

CHAPTER 3

The Carpetbagger Governor

Much of the South was in a bad way following the end of the Civil War, and Dade County was no exception. It was a time for the Southern states to recover and renew, and it was a time when black citizens needed to be encouraged and strengthened. Unfortunately, widespread greed and racism still prevailed. In an era when Northern carpetbaggers and Southern scalawags were looking to make financial gains and to preserve white sovereignty, both groups would be considered jerks in the opinion of most people in the twenty-first century, and surely W. H. Gleason would stand out among them all.

Born in Richford, New York, in 1829, William Henry Gleason trained as a lawyer and as an engineer before he moved to Wisconsin. There he was instrumental in founding the town named Eau Claire, but he left the details of helping the town to advance to others. He held the position as president of the town's first bank, the Bank of Eau Claire, while he learned the ins and outs of the real estate business and was an increasingly influential operative in the Democratic Party, all before he was thirty years old. While he and his wife, Sarah, made their home and started their family, he went on to open bank after bank in several other states when he could spare some time from his dealings in real estate development. By the age of thirty-six, he was said to have already acquired and lost a fortune and was well on his way to acquiring a second one.

People who knew him said Gleason had a remarkable way of looking at things, in that "he no sooner saw a conception of his own under way, than he seemed to lose interest in it and flit to a new one."

However, his reputation as a go-getter was slightly tarnished when rumors circulated that charges in bank speculation had

William H. Gleason

been brought against him, and in addition, he was involved in more than one suspect business transaction. Moreover, during the time when he was a legal vote-counter, he submitted votes for a township in which there had been no election. The indomitable Gleason succeeded in ignoring all charges and simply moved on.

Never one to miss out on an opportunity, during the Civil War, Gleason and W. H. Hunt, a special friend of his, acted as sutlers, which meant they followed various branches of the army, selling provisions to the soldiers, a lucrative undertaking. Hunt would join Gleason in various other ventures over the years.

Then in 1865, the Freedman's Bureau appointed Gleason to be a special agent. In that capacity and without pay, he accompanied George F. Thompson, the inspector for the Bureau of Freedmen, Refugees and Abandoned Lands, on a tour of lightly settled south Florida to check out possible locations for the establishment of a Negro colony. That colony never came to be, but while the two men found nothing of interest on the west coast, Gleason was much impressed with the subtropical Biscayne Bay area and its potential for future opportunities. The major complaint Thompson wrote about in his report concerned the insects, warning that "mosquitoes and sand flies seem to vie with each other in their efforts to torment humanity."

Gleason, however, was not deterred. Six months later, he rented a schooner to haul his wife, Sarah, and their two sons, his friend W. H. Hunt, and the Hunt family—plus several workmen with their heavy equipment, including mowing machines and assorted animals—to Dade County, to the abandoned Fort Dallas military buildings. The families brought seeds to plant and basic foods to last them for six months. Hunt brought along an actual printing press, possibly hoping to launch a newspaper, but that would have to be put on hold for a while as there were only about thirty or forty people living in Dade County. Hunt also unloaded what almost amounted to a library of books, many of which would be helpful to them in their unfamiliar new surroundings.

The families joined the few other stouthearted souls who made up the population in the entire county, one of whom watched

Gleason's schooner being unloaded and described it to friends as a veritable Noah's ark.

Hunt and Gleason planted hay and other crops, but Gleason, never one to sit and watch the hay grow, became involved in investing in land under the control of Florida's Internal Improvement Fund. He proposed digging ditches to drain the land in exchange for having the opportunity to purchase real estate rights at bargain prices—six cents an acre, in one instance.

In 1868, he paid $1.25 per acre for sixteen thousand acres of land on Florida's east central coast. Observing the coquina rocks scattering the shore, he named the area Eau Gallie, meaning "rocky water" in French. Gleason offered 2,320 acres of his property to the State of Florida to establish an agricultural college. He had a two-story classroom building constructed on the land, but as the result of Reconstruction politics, the plans were changed and the college was relocated first to Lake City, then to Gainesville, eventually becoming the University of Florida. Ever the opportunist, years later, Gleason would turn his empty building into the Grenada Hotel.

He spent a great deal of his time traveling between Dade County and Tallahassee, in Leon County. During his travels he made friends in politics and in business, some of them Republicans with power. Never one to ignore a possible advantage, he decided to convert to the Republican Party.

Harrison Reed, a Republican described as being another carpetbagger from Wisconsin, won the office of governor in 1868. With some help from his new influential associates, W. H. Gleason was designated to be Reed's lieutenant governor, only the second one in the recently created position in Florida.

The new lieutenant governor's best friend, W. H. Hunt, became Dade County's senator, and it is most likely safe to assume Gleason also exerted some influence when the governor appointed the other new officers for Dade County.

Governor Reed had lived a long time in Florida. He was a Union Army doctor and ran the *Union-Republican* newspaper in Jacksonville at one time. Apparently, at first he made sincere attempts to encourage cooperation among the three parties—the radical Republicans, who were mostly carpetbaggers and supporters of blacks; the Democrats, who were Crackers and former Confederates; and the conservative Republicans, who, like the governor, attempted to stay in the center—with little success.

Gleason gradually and quietly allied himself with several of the more radical legislators. Together they came up with a scheme to exchange state bonds for worthless scrip (a certificate indicating payment will be made later, mostly granted to government employees) and provide impressive profits. The legislators had planned to include the governor in the resulting windfall, but Reed apparently experienced a twinge of conscience and was uncomfortable with the scheme. Without his backing, the plan went nowhere, which further widened the growing gap between the governor and his lieutenant governor.

Reed also summoned enough nerve to veto a bill that would have raised legislators' salaries, and most likely that was the last straw. A group led by Gleason prepared articles of impeachment against Governor Reed. The legislature adjourned without holding a trial, but Gleason knew an opportunity when he saw one, and he declared himself to be the governor of Florida. Undeterred by Reed aides who blocked access to the governor's office, Gleason brazenly set up his own office in a hotel directly across the street from the capitol. When he made an attempt to pick up some papers from Reed's office one day, a Reed supporter threatened him with a revolver, a strong-arm tactic even Gleason could not ignore.

He was fortunate to have the cooperation of the secretary of state, George J. Alden, who removed the state seal from his office and turned it over to the "new governor" in order to give the seal of authenticity to all the documents Gleason signed during the months of November and December in 1868. For nearly two months, Florida had two men calling themselves governor, which might have been an early indication that "things are different down here," as a television commercial would proclaim many years later.

Governor Reed finally had enough. He petitioned the State Supreme Court for an opinion on his impeachment and received the answer he wanted. The court declared him still the governor, and as such, he challenged Gleason's right to his office. Reed was backed by some of his friends on the State Supreme Court. Then, in addition, Gleason was belatedly disqualified as lieutenant governor owing to the fact that he had not been a Florida resident for three years before election—a legal requirement that had originally been intended to keep blacks out of office.

Gleason was officially removed from office in December 1868, but even that didn't slow him down for long. The eight or ten folks who lived in Dade County in the early 1870s were supposed to be represented by a state legislator, but no one had bothered to organize an election, and as a result, no one had ever been elected to the legislature. When Gleason learned of the situation, he swiftly elected himself and journeyed to Tallahassee, where he was unchallenged. During Gleason's time in office, an acquaintance stated that "he offered more bills in the legislature for internal improvements than any other man living or dead had ever done before."

Gleason held the office from 1870 to the election in 1874, when he lost the seat by two votes. That didn't stop him either. Since he was county commissioner, county clerk, and county judge, and on the board of canvassers, he was unimpeded and continued to reward the members of the legislature with his presence. In fact, Gleason held half the offices in Dade County, while his friends or sympathetic associates held the other half.

Holding those three notable positions in Dade County enabled Gleason to make his presence felt in various ways and at the same time to make money doing it. Dade County's yearly income was only in the neighborhood of $300 per year, but in one year the county paid Gleason $100 for his salary as county clerk and another $120 for his survey of a road, which was not built until thirty years later.

Although Gleason was more annoying than a cloud of mosquitoes to some Floridians, he was tolerated by others because, without question, he led everyone else in drawing new settlers to the Dade region at a time when the area sorely needed to attract more citizens. His name was frequently mentioned in promotional material—guidebooks and travel books. In the *Guide Book to Florida,* it was stated that "Lieutenant Governor Gleason resides at Miami and will entertain travelers to the extent that he can."

Another guidebook quoted Gleason as saying, "The pure water and other mineral springs, the magnificent beauty of its scenery, the salubrity and equability of its climate, must make Biscayne Bay at no distant day, the resort of the tourist and the lover of adventure." That must have enticed a few settlers.

The accolades continued, with an official in the Committee of Lands and Immigration reporting the following: "Whatever impetus immigration to this portion of the state (Dade County) has received has been due to the energy and the enterprise of the Hon. W. G. Gleason, who is permanently located at Miami and is thoroughly identified with the material prosperity of the state and particularly Dade County."

There were those who believed that Gleason wanted to develop Florida "not only for benevolent reasons," because if land could be drained and sold to newcomers, he would gain financially in a big way. He would not be the last to subscribe to that idea.

One new citizen who did not agree that Gleason was doing more good than harm was Dr. Jephta Harris. In 1869 he bought a large section of the Fort Dallas property, contending that Gleason's and Hunt's claim of owning a US government lease to the land was invalid. After a great deal of controversy, Gleason and Hunt simply gave up and moved farther north to the area now called Miami Shores. They did not go quietly, as might be expected. They took the post office with them and renamed it "Biscayne," and therefore legally, Miami did not actually exist from 1870 to 1874.

Gleason didn't give up on the Fort Dallas property either. Somehow he learned there had been a misspelling of the name on the original grant in 1824. Through some convoluted maneuvering, he managed to buy title to the property in his wife's name. Enraged, Dr. Harris contacted the government in Washington, DC, with charges of fraud and also threatened to shoot and "take care" of Gleason in a duel. The bad feelings didn't quite come to that, but some time later, Harris did physically attack Gleason on a street in Key West, to the obvious pleasure of several onlookers. Gleason's reputation as a jerk seemed to be spreading, but as usual, he was undaunted.

He made his presence known in other interesting ways. At the time, Broward and Dade Counties together sent one senator to the legislature. It was 1876, and the Centennial of the Declaration of Independence aroused more than the usual election excitement. Outside of Florida, people were chattering about the feverish contest between Rutherford B. Hayes and Samuel J. Tilden for the office of president of the United States. Inside Dade County, the seventy-three registered voters were more concerned with local matters. One local contest was between Israel Stewart and John Varnum, and the other had John J. Brown running against William H. Gleason.

Dade County had three precincts: a lonely one in Jupiter, set up mainly for its lighthouse keepers; one in Lake Worth; and one called Sears Precinct, long-established at the home of a man named Sears. It was there at the Sears precinct that three votes cast by foreign sailors were challenged by poll workers. The sailors claimed to have previously filed the necessary papers in the capitol at Tallahassee, indicating their "declaration of intention" to become United States citizens. At that time any voter who possessed a "declaration of intention" was permitted to vote. One inspector admitted to having the declarations of the three sailors in an office in Biscayne. He generously told the sailors he would deliver them if they would promise to vote the way he told them.

Not unexpectedly, there was quite a ruckus, but a boat was sent to Biscayne to pick up the papers and return with them. It took some time, but authorities kept the polls open until the boat returned and the three sailors voted.

The vote counting began, with bystanders as witnesses. An unexpected wind blew (or it was suggested that possibly a discreet bystander might have waved something or other to cause a breeze) and fifteen or twenty ballots scattered to the ground, but they were rescued by onlookers and included in the count. At the final tally, Gleason lost. To the surprise of no one at this point, he contested the election.

The residents of Dade County neither knew about the outcome of the general election, nor would they have cared if they had known. But not only was there an undecided election in Dade County, the result in the national contest between Hayes and Tilden was just as controversial. Finally, it came down to where Tilden needed only one more electoral vote to be declared the winner, but there were three states whose results were not yet returned: Florida, South Carolina, and Louisiana.

In Florida, Hayes appeared to have a slim lead, but Dade County's results were not yet in. As the nation waited for the results in the national election, Gleason took his case to the Dade County canvassers. He insisted that the Sears precinct had been the scene of illegal voting, including, he said, someone who had voted after dark and another person who attempted to vote but did not have proper papers. Certainly, he insisted, when the ballots fell to the ground, someone had altered a number of them. Gleason had eight pages of sworn statements by supporters indicating that illegal voting had gone on.

In the end, the canvassers decided to eliminate all the votes from the Sears precinct, and at the final count, William H. Gleason won his election with just seven votes. The winner not only delivered the Dade County returns to Tallahassee, and the county to the Republicans, he assured Hayes of a presidential victory even though it had already become apparent that Hayes had won. It was, however, the earliest beginning of the ongoing Florida election jokes.

Elections over, the new legislature, controlled by Democrats, denied Gleason his seat in the senate. Being that he was also losing influence in Dade County, he decided to move permanently to Eau Gallie in Brevard County. While he established a boat building business and a sawmill there, he took over the lands he still had and the deserted building he still owned, the one that had been planned for the agricultural college but never materialized. He lived there with his wife and sons for some time. After extended legal maneuvering with the Florida State Agricultural College, Gleason paid them two thousand dollars for the small, empty building and the land surrounding it, which he would eventually turn into the moneymaking Grenada Hotel. The hotel was demolished in a fire a few years later.

Gleason spent the rest of his life in a beautiful home he built for his family in Eau Gallie. He died there in 1902. William H. Gleason was a Florida resident who certainly qualified as a jerk in much of his behavior but who, on the other hand, did much to entice needed settlers to the empty land. His sons, William and George, followed in their father's footsteps, operating a land development business.

Before his wife, Sarah, died in 1912, she arranged for a mile-long piece of Gleason property along the Atlantic Ocean to be preserved as a park for public use. To this day, beachgoers who enjoy access to the beautiful sand and surf owe their thanks to the jerk, his wife, and their heirs.

CHAPTER 4

Florida's Green Menace

Like any other state in the United States, Florida has always had its share of scoundrels, swindlers, and other jerks who habitually break the law, make shady deals, and commit murder and mayhem. But no individual was responsible for the widespread havoc and destruction Florida witnessed for many decades. Indeed, the damage was not done by a human being at all. The real jerk in this case was a deceptively beautiful plant.

In 1884, the city of New Orleans played host to an assemblage that would have a massive and long-lasting effect not only on the state of Louisiana but also on her neighbor, the Sunshine State. The occasion was known as the New Orleans World's Fair, but its official name was the World's Industrial and Cotton Centennial Exposition.

For some unknown reason, the organization representing Japan decided to give attractive plants known as water hyacinths as gifts to their visitors. Why the Japanese had chosen to give away water hyacinths, a plant that originated in South America, no one knows for sure; but their apparent act of goodwill would result in a worldwide problem that emanated from the spread of the purple plant. Among the many people who took home the lovely plants was Mrs. W. F. Fuller.

Mr. and Mrs. W. F. Fuller lived comfortably in the Palatka area in the late 1880s and owned citrus groves, which were located along the St. Johns River in Putman County. Mrs. Fuller was so taken with the beauty of her new plant, which she received as a gift, that she wanted to show it off in the fish pond in her yard. She had no idea how threatening a pretty plant could become.

Water hyacinths are floating plants with smooth, glossy, bright green leaves and flowers with six purplish petals, and if ever a plant could be classified as a jerk, this one could. What Mrs. Fuller

Water hyacinths on the St. Johns River
STATE ARCHIVES OF FLORIDA, FLORIDA MEMORY, HTTP://FLORIDAMEMORY.COM/ITEMS/SHOW/37983

didn't know when she put her plant in her fish pond was that water hyacinths spread rapidly. She did note that the plant quickly overwhelmed her pond, which might have been alarming to someone familiar with invasive plant species. Instead, Mrs. Fuller simply thinned them out and then made her second mistake, this one a far-reaching one. Her husband helped her to get rid of the excess plants by tossing them into the water off the family dock located on the St. Johns River, the longest river in Florida. Mr. Fuller, who owned the Edgewater Grove, a few miles north of Palatka, came to believe the people of Florida owed him and his wife a debt of gratitude for bringing such beautiful flowers to the state. And in fact, Mrs. Fuller let it be known that in her opinion, the water hyacinths would be a great improvement over the uninteresting greenery without flowers that usually floated on Florida waters. However, soon after the Fullers beautified their waters, two hundred miles of the St. Johns River were pronounced unnavigable due to the hyacinth proliferation.

Another member of the unenlightened was Eli Morgan, a well-known cattleman and upstanding citizen of Manatee County, who at one time was described as a "cattle king." The owner of twenty thousand head of beef cattle, Morgan spent a great deal of his time fighting cattle rustlers. In the late 1800s, the Wild West was more famous for such action, but it had nothing on the Florida ranches, where the danger from rustlers was ever-present. In his spare time, Morgan also owned and managed a ten-room hotel.

When Morgan happened to see the water hyacinths in the St. Johns River, he appreciated their beautiful appearance, but what really excited him was the possibility of using the plants to feed his twenty thousand head of cattle. He brought some of the plants to his area, tossed them into the water, and as a result, was responsible for launching the water hyacinth into the Kissimmee River.

Like the Fullers, Morgan didn't take the time to learn anything about the South American blossoms before he introduced them to the waters of his part of the continent. Within a decade, water hyacinths blanketed an estimated fifty million acres of the St. Johns River and its tributaries. From the Kissimmee River in the center of the state, the plants traveled south to Lake Okeechobee, then on to the Everglades and throughout the rest of south Florida. Moreover, Eli Morgan learned too late that water hyacinths are 96 percent water and that to depend on them as the sole feed for cattle would result in the animals starving to death.

The water hyacinth has since legitimately become known as the world's worst water weed, able to double its mass every five days if conditions are favorable. Even worse, its seeds remain viable for at least twenty years.

Although the lovely purple flowers last just a day or two, when they have finished blooming, their stalks bend, lowering the faded flowers and their seed pods into the water, where the pods release the seeds. Under the water, the feathery, fibrous roots can extend out as far as two feet, forming mats. In addition, the hyacinths are freshwater plants much at home in Florida, since the plants are killed when they reach salt water and are also killed by frosts.

Considered the world's worst weed, the water hyacinths inflict havoc in so many ways: They block channels and rivers, interfere with livestock's access to drinking water, destroy native water plants on which some animals depend for their homes, and reduce penetration of sunlight, thus changing the oxygen level, temperature, and pH of waters. The increased temperature causes fish to disappear, and in some places, snakes and crocodiles have increased their presence.

The impenetrable water hyacinth mats also hamper recreation in the water passages and ruin the aesthetic value of the waterways. The huge mats frequently break and float off, destroying roads, fences, and even crops and pastures. Some large hydropower plants have developed problems shown to be due to the presence of water hyacinths in local waters.

In the late 1800s, when the earth's worst aquatic weed was introduced to Florida, the St. Johns River was the main commercial passageway through the 310 miles of wilderness, while the East Coast Railroad was the main north–south land route. Crossing the St. Johns to the north, near Palatka, the East Coast Railroad bridge was about to be extensively rebuilt. Except at the center where ships passed through, the original bridge pilings had planks installed, which extended from one piling to the next, almost at the surface of the water. Depending on the direction of the wind, the hyacinths would collect at the planking to form an impassable mat except for the clear waters at the center, where ships were forced to line up to pass through. When winds persisted for days, even the center of the river could become obstructed.

The citizens of Palatka banded together to explain the situation to the East Coast Railroad authorities, pleading with them to have changes made in the bridge construction and to do away with the old type of planks at the pilings, in order to allow the hyacinth mats to pass through the channel without being blocked. The railroad officials agreed to begin to alter the existing bracing during routine maintenance.

That problem would be addressed, but there still remained thousands of acres of plants in the waters, doubling their mass every five days.

In 1897, an engineer, John Warren Sackett, opened a base just north of Sanford to conduct experiments in controlling the increasingly problematic water hyacinth. He focused on the three available forces that might be used in the effort: natural, chemical, and mechanical.

It was well known that man had already made several ghastly mistakes by introducing nonnative plants and animals to fight invasive pests in other regions of the world, so Sackett thought it best to rule out the natural effort.

Beginning his experiments with chemicals, Sackett first tried spraying plants with a 50 percent solution of muriatic acid. When that proved ineffectual, he increased it to a 100 percent solution. In one month, the plants faded temporarily but then quickly rebounded and were as healthy as before. Similar results followed sprays of carbolic acid, and then sulfuric acid. An attempt was made to use high-pressure spraying, which caused plants to shred temporarily but then to regrow as if nothing had happened. Even efforts at burning plants doused with kerosene produced only temporary damage.

Sackett decided it was time to move on to mechanical methods. Using a planing mill roller such as is used in the steel and woodworking industries, he achieved some success in crushing the plants. However, when he attempted to tow plant mats to the rollers, he was met with great difficulty if the wind or currents were unfavorable.

Since the best effect resulted from the crushing rollers, two boats were designed to be built. They were to be equipped with mechanisms to pull the "green menace," as water hyacinths were becoming known, toward the rollers to be crushed. One boat was built and sent to Louisiana to see how effective it would be. Sackett was sufficiently disappointed with the results of that operation that he canceled construction of the boat that had been intended for Florida.

While that was going on, Harvesta Chemical Compounding Company, a New Orleans chemical company, developed a spray for which it had high hopes for use in the water hyacinth war. Florida engineers received the go-ahead to try the spray on an area at Bridgeport, along the west bank of the St. Johns River just north of Palatka. Hopes were raised when the sprayed green menace plants died within five to seven days, then continued to decompose as they floated away, offering no problem to passing boats. Not only was the cost reasonable, but cattlemen were elated to hear that a wandering cow had eaten the freshly sprayed plants and exhibited no untoward symptoms at all—a very good sign.

Meanwhile, engineers, having been so frequently disappointed, continued to try other chemicals with varying results. Florida engineers equipped a houseboat previously rented out for private parties with a pump, hoses, and other equipment needed to spray three thousand gallons of a chemical with the chief active ingredient being arsenic acid. In six months, the houseboat, *Le Reve,* sprayed 242,503 gallons of the chemical from Palatka to Lake Jessup but stopped the tests when cattlemen objected.

Some of the methods, including those conducted from the *Le Reve,* resulted in complaints that cattle were dying from eating sprayed plants, and eventually the cattlemen took their complaints to Congress. In 1905, Florida stopped all spraying of the green menace, and a search for a solution was begun at a new test station under the direction of Major Francis R. Shrunk.

In order to try to make peace with cattlemen, Shrunk looked for a way to keep cattle away from the sprayed hyacinths. He experimented with various substances including cow manure, aloe, whale oil soap, and finally with water containing decomposed egg. The smelly egg seemed to work, and the cattle stayed away from the sprayed plants. Unfortunately, after eight successful days, a severe storm washed the treated plants away along with the test results.

None of the attempted experiments proved to be very impressive, so for the next thirty years, mechanical removal took precedence, even though it was not the magic bullet everyone was hoping to discover.

In the meantime, the green menace spread to Florida's west coast rivers, and south to Lake Okechobee, the largest lake in the United States after the Great Lakes, and on down into the newly built drainage canals. The Sunshine State's waterways were filled with water hyacinths.

During this time, and on until 1939, mechanical removal was considered the most effective available tool in weed warfare. An improved sawboat was used to cut the plants into wide strips and then shred them so that they fell into the water and decomposed. The boat was an effective killer, but it was being asked to solve an overwhelming and far-flung catastrophe. One notable example of its effectiveness was when the sawboat removed 1,617,427 square yards of water hyacinth mats from the St. Johns River at the tiny town of Astor.

Other methods were continually being tried. Besides the sawboats, in some places draglines pulled mats to the shore, bulldozers worked the firmer marshes, men sawed jammed plants away from bridge trestles, and sometimes timber saws were employed where it was feasible.

By 1939, it was obvious that mechanical methods were inadequate. Engineers began another system in which plant traps were set up along channels to maneuver plants away from the channel to where they could be destroyed. Floating booms installed across the mouths of river branches prevented plants from invading farther upstream.

Another method that was attempted was to place diseased, worm-infested plants in among healthy water hyacinths, hoping to spread the disease. This method failed when the blight did not spread to the healthy plants.

All of these methods became increasingly important with the beginning of World War II, when US Navy seaplanes stationed in Florida required the open waters on the St. Johns River to operate.

The war effort was also the impetus for the discovery of 2, 4-D (2, 4-dichlorphenoxyl acetic acid), a weed killer that much later would be used as an ingredient in Agent Orange. When World War II ended, 2, 4-D was tested on water hyacinths in Florida with gratifying success. In addition, aerial surveillance with military helicopters was begun, which made it easy to identify large trouble spots and quickly spray them from above. Airboats that could ride over plants were also helpful, as they were able to get into and spray areas that previously had been unreachable.

It was almost eighty years after Mr. and Mrs. Fuller tossed their excess water hyacinth plants into the St. Johns River that Putnam County officials were sufficiently satisfied with the progress that had been made against the invasive species that they requested a limit to the spraying of the region near Palatka. The engineers agreed and removed their heavy equipment from the area. However, it was soon discovered that many large mats had been blown downstream, causing heavy damage to docks and piers and killing fish.

After several welcome frosts burned the mats during the following winter, a new effort against the green menace, dubbed "Operation Clean Sweep," was begun. By that time, engineers recognized how important it was to stay ahead of the plants, and to prevent them from overtaking tributaries with matted jams rather than attacking them after they gained a foothold. Year-round spraying—rather than spraying after jams were already formed—was more effective in maintaining control.

The US Army Corps of Engineers had not yet given up trying to find safe, economical methods of water hyacinth control. They brought some of the water hyacinth weevil (*Neochetina eichorniae*) from Argentina, quarantined them for a time, and then introduced them to plants in Fort Lauderdale, Florida. The weevils matured, dined on the unwelcome plants, and spread to make their homes in every sizable green menace habitat.

A few years later, the hyacinth moth (*Sameodes albiguttalis*) was installed among the plants to join the battle in twenty different Florida regions. The first attempt to establish colonies of the moths failed, but engineers had better luck the following year. The moths were added to the arsenal in the battle against the green menace.

However, the water hyacinth is not the only invasive exotic that is of concern, and Florida is not its only victim. Although Hawaii has suffered from water hyacinth infestation more than any other place, Florida is known to be the recipient of two thousand invasive species, mostly plants and insects. International shipping has become a major cause of the problem. It is estimated that about forty thousand gallons of ballast water is discharged into water along the United States coast every minute. Along with foreign plants, Florida's waters continue to receive nonnative reptiles, amphibians, and mollusks.

Not surprisingly, a total elimination of the water hyacinth is not expected ever to be achieved, but the situation is now considered to be under control.

CHAPTER 5

The Burning of Styx

It might seem a bit of a stretch to call a man like Henry Flagler a jerk. After all, he left his home in New York when he was just fourteen years old to lessen his father's financial burden of providing for their large family. The teenager made his way all alone to Ohio, where he finished growing up and then married a distant cousin, Mary Harkness. He partnered with John D. Rockefeller to launch the number-one industrial power of the time, the Standard Oil Company. Most people would have been satisfied to claim that as their life's work, but Flagler moved on to Florida, where he was in large part responsible for opening up the entire southeast coast of the state to tourism. At his death he left behind endowments to Florida colleges and hospitals and even some newspapers, which had not been especially kind to him while he was alive. His spectacular accomplishments, however, did not excuse his behavior at other times when the so-called robber baron behaved like a jerk.

Henry Morrison Flagler was born in 1830 in Hopewell, New York, into a family of half-brothers and half-sisters and a thrice-married preacher father. His best boyhood pal was Dan Harkness, a half-brother, but in 1838, Dan moved away to join the other side of his family in Ohio. In order to relieve his father of providing for him, fourteen-year-old Henry decided to make his way to Ohio too. There Dan introduced him to Dan's other family and their business, the Harkness general store.

The two boys remained close during the time when Henry was learning the ins and outs of running the Harkness store. He discovered that not only did he have a liking for sales and business, he seemed to have a real knack for it as well.

During the same time that Dan courted and married his distant cousin, Isabella, Henry was falling in love with Isabella's

Street scene at the Styx, Palm Beach, Florida, in 1895
STATE ARCHIVES OF FLORIDA, FLORIDA MEMORY, HTTP://FLORIDAMEMORY.COM/ITEMS/SHOW/118079

sister, Mary, and they married in 1853. The newlyweds set up housekeeping in Mary's hometown, Bellevue, Ohio.

Mary's family made Henry Flagler a partner in the Bellevue firm, Harkness and Company, which shipped substantial quantities of wheat to Cleveland, where John D. Rockefeller was managing the shipments. Before long, Flagler moved his family to Cleveland, Ohio. Flagler and Rockefeller, who shared an intense desire to achieve financial success, formed a deep friendship that would last all their lives.

At that time, the petroleum industry was developing rapidly. Rockefeller, who had invested in it early, formed a business partnership with Flagler, which in a few years would be called the Standard Oil Company. It was the beginning of a long, comfortable life for Henry Flagler. Standard Oil would go on to monopolize the entire American oil industry and hold on to its position for a long time.

Rockefeller always openly credited his partner with the rapid progress the company made in its early days, particularly with initiating the move to buy up smaller companies, which forced struggling competitors out of business and essentially created a monopoly. While Flagler was known to insist his workers be treated fairly, it was not beneath him and Rockefeller to find ways to pressure railroads to agree to give Standard Oil advantages over their smaller competitors, thus forcing them out of business. Flagler was exhibiting decidedly jerk-like behavior, which triggered frequent scathing newspaper articles and even resulted in both him and Rockefeller being burned in effigy.

Standard Oil Company moved its headquarters to New York City in 1877, and Flagler, then the secretary of the corporation, felt he, too, should make the move with his family.

By then, Mary and Henry's family consisted of two daughters, Jennie Louise and Carrie, and one son, Harry Harkness, but Carrie died when she was just three years old. Mary Flagler's health, which had always been fragile, continued to worsen, with her main difficulties centered in her respiratory system. Her doctors recommended that she spend time in Florida with the warm sun and the bracing sea air.

Except for the most northern part of the state, the Florida peninsula was still mostly unsettled, and although Flagler assumed the worst about the territory, he reluctantly agreed to the journey. Clearly, his expectations were fulfilled, for after they reached Savannah, Georgia, the rest of the trip became increasingly uncomfortable and difficult for them.

Stopping first in Jacksonville, they enjoyed the wonderful climate but quickly became bored with the scant diversions and inconvenient distance from the beach. Next they traveled to mosquito-plagued St. Augustine, which Flagler called a "pesthole." They then took the first train back to Jacksonville, where Flagler rated the accommodations and food very bad and complained that most of the visitors were consumptives. He described Jacksonville as awful and decided to return to New York after a few weeks. Mary would not stay in Florida without him, no matter what her doctors said, and her husband refused to remain there.

Back in New York, the cold weather appeared to aggravate Mary's breathing problems, but she refused to return to Florida alone, and Henry insisted he must remain available for Standard Oil business. It was a major decision that to most people unquestionably certified him as a jerk; he would have to live with his choice for the rest of his life.

Mary's health continued to deteriorate, requiring Flagler to hire a full-time caregiver for her, a former actress, Ida Alice Shourds. The Flaglers' daughter, Jennie Louise, now a married woman, helped as much as she could with the household, but Flagler talked his half-sister Carrie into moving to New York to run his home and help look after his eleven-year-old son, Harry. Flagler stayed at Mary's bedside until her death in 1881, deeply affected by the loss of his great love and, some said, by feelings of guilt for not remaining in Florida when her health had been so precarious.

Shortly before Mary's death, Henry had rented a thirty-two-acre estate on Long Island with a huge forty-room mansion and several guest houses. When he worked at Standard Oil headquarters in the city, he spent weekdays at his hotel in Manhattan and then filled his weekends entertaining family and friends on Long Island. He was also beginning to be seen in the company of Mary's former caregiver, Ida Alice.

After some time, Flagler bought the Long Island estate he had been renting, and on June 5, 1883, he and Ida Alice were married. Standard Oil business kept Flagler occupied until December, when the newlyweds were able to enjoy a delayed honeymoon in Florida's sunny weather, while a cold spell froze their friends up north.

By that time, Flagler was getting bored with Standard Oil business and was looking for new challenges. He was impressed to see how St. Augustine had changed for the better since he had been there previously. Although accommodations had vastly improved, he considered the existing hotels average at best and began to mull over the idea of building a really fine hotel in the area. Before he and Ida Alice left for home, Flagler purchased some Florida property and began forming plans and making preparations to construct the best hotel in America.

He spared no expense in building his showplace of cement and coquina shell, installing some windows by Tiffany and providing electricity by four Edison direct current dynamos. It turned out to be truly the hotel he envisioned, a place for people of wealth, with excellent food and fine music. He named it the Ponce de Leon and was so pleased with it that he immediately started to build another smaller, less-expensive hotel for guests who desired an ocean view. Situated across from the Ponce de Leon, the smaller hotel was called the Alcazar.

Flagler reserved a suite at the Ponce de Leon as his and Ida Alice's permanent winter home until their new winter home, which they called Kirkside, in St. Augustine, was completed. A luxurious private rail car hauled them back and forth between New York and Florida.

Recalling the unpleasant travel experience he and Mary had on their first trip south, Flagler concluded it would be essential to provide decent, comfortable transportation for his hotel guests. Considering the extent of his Standard Oil wealth, that would not be a problem. He purchased several small rail lines and then proceeded to have workers lay track into new, unserved areas, south to Daytona and on to Palm Beach, where he started construction on a new Royal Poinciana Hotel.

While he was enjoying his new career outside of the Standard Oil business, Ida Alice was enjoying his money and social prestige. She tried to gain acceptance into New York's high society when they lived at their Long Island home or at Kirkside when they wintered in St. Augustine, but despite her husband's reputation, she had little success. Even though she held elaborate balls, which were attended by hundreds of guests, and wore extravagant gowns and dazzling jewels, she was never truly accepted. Flagler joined her affairs for a time, but eventually, he lost interest and would leave the parties early to retire.

During this time, Ida Alice began exhibiting increasingly erratic behavior that most definitely was not normal. Her flashes of temper over small incidents frequently turned into loud rages. She gossiped, not always truthfully, about socially well-known acquaintances and about her husband's infidelities.

When an unnamed friend gave her a Ouija board, Ida Alice seemed to step over the line into complete madness. She communed with ghosts and began to avoid Flagler, telling her friends that she planned to kill him and marry the Czar of Russia, who— she said—was madly in love with her. After Flagler had his new wife examined by prominent specialists, who pronounced her hopelessly insane, he knew what he had to do.

Flagler had his wife institutionalized at Choate's Sanitarium in Pleasantville, New York, where she remained for the rest of her life. He set up a generous fund for her care.

Although Ida Alice was certainly delusional where the Czar of Russia was concerned, it would appear there was some basis for her complaints of Flagler's infidelities. He was named in a New York divorce suit, reportedly bought a townhouse for another woman, and at some time openly took up with a young, attractive socialite, Mary Lily Kenan. When Ida Alice was institutionalized in 1897, Flagler spent more and more time with Mary Lily.

Earlier, in the late 1880s, while cruising south on his yacht, Flagler had discovered and been charmed by an island called Palm Beach, which was bordered on one side by the Atlantic Ocean and on the other by Lake Worth. Immediately, he began to make plans. He thought it would be a perfect locale for another hotel—a very special hotel. And the railway would have to be extended for guests to reach it. He had originally intended to stop his railway at Daytona, but Palm Beach became the new destination. He began to buy up tracts of land and made plans to build the world's largest hotel.

It was an exciting time in Flagler's life. His work in opening up Florida to tourists with his railway and his hotels pleased him much more than the office work in New York; and he became determined to marry Mary Lily.

The problem was that he was still married to Ida Alice; in the state of New York, where he was still a resident, the only grounds for divorce was adultery. Being that Ida Alice was locked up in an asylum, there was no way he could use that. However, for Henry Flagler it was not a problem. The unstoppable robber baron changed his legal residence from New York to Florida, and meanwhile he pulled strings to have the New York Supreme Court declare Ida Alice legally insane. As in New York, Florida's grounds for divorce was adultery, but Flagler, the man who was opening up the state to tourism by building railways and hotels, had connections few ordinary people would ever have. He not only controlled Florida transportation and all major construction, he essentially called the signals at the main newspapers and in Florida politics.

Two and a half weeks after a bill was introduced in the Florida senate making incurable insanity grounds for divorce, the bill passed; on April 25 Governor William Jennings signed it into law. Flagler filed for divorce on August 13, 1901, and married Mary Lily on August 24, 1901. Flagler's was the only divorce ever granted under the law, which was repealed four years later.

Suspicions of bribery were widespread, but officially no evidence of bribery was uncovered until seventy years later, when researchers received permission to view Florida East Coast Railroad files that had previously been unavailable. Names of prominent legislators, dates, and other items in the files strongly indicate Henry Flagler made substantial pay-offs, once more qualifying him to be considered a jerk.

Even so, it must have been difficult to make the enormous decisions required for his far-flung business operations while his personal life was in such disarray. Besides his marital difficulties, he was profoundly saddened when Jennie, the second daughter from his first marriage, died. In addition, he and his only son were not close and finally severed their relationship because the son refused to follow in his father's footsteps and join in his organization.

Flagler buried himself in his business affairs and in building a magnificent new fifty-five-room mansion for himself and his new bride. Mary Lily called it a marble palace, and they named it Whitehall.

While the development of Florida fed Flagler's ego, he was sincerely gratified to be making important contributions to civilization. Not only was he responsible for hotels and railroads, he also provided St. Augustine with a hospital, a city hall, a school for blacks, and three churches.

He began construction on the massive new hotel in Palm Beach, to be called the Royal Poinciana. It would indeed be the largest hotel in the world, with accommodations for two thousand guests and a staff of between twelve hundred and sixteen hundred, prepared to coddle the expected cream of high society. Flagler wanted the hotel to be built of wood with as much speed as possible in order to have it finished when the next leg of his East Coast Railroad would reach Palm Beach.

The Royal Poinciana, fronting on Lake Worth, opened in 1894, and then in order to please guests who desired ocean frontage, Flagler built another hotel, the Breakers, which he opened in 1896.

By this point in his life, Henry Flagler had not only set off a real estate boom by buying land for his railroad and for his hotels, he also became a major employer in the area, hiring fifteen hundred men to lay his tracks and another one thousand men to build his Palm Beach hotel.

He also made a point to pay his workers better than workers in other similar jobs. Many of his workers were blacks, who were happy for their jobs even though there were no housing facilities for them. Most of them followed the unauthorized rule of the day, "Squatters' Rights," which meant they cleared a piece of the jungle-like land belonging to no one and claimed that plot as their own. There was no running water, no sanitary facilities, no garbage hauling. Approximately two thousand blacks called their community of tents and shacks the Styx, which, perhaps prophetically, was the name of the river in Greek mythology that led to hell.

Whether or not Flagler's role in the demolishment of the Styx is actual truth or a legend, it has endured for more than a hundred years and if true, would suggest once more that he did occasionally qualify as a jerk.

As the hotel construction progressed, there was not enough living space for all the workers on the island, but plenty of unoccupied land existed on the mainland. Flagler believed it would be a good idea to move Styx to the mainland and establish a new town there "for my help," as he said. That way, the Astors, the Wanamakers, the Vanderbilts, and their friends would not be exposed to the visible harsh conditions of the Styx on the otherwise beautiful island. Accordingly, in 1893 Flagler purchased several hundred acres of property on the mainland, to be called West Palm Beach.

In addition, he hoped the move would quiet complaints from other white property owners who had flocked into the area and were complaining about the "unsavory locality" and "the horribly unsanitary conditions" of the Styx and insisting the "deadly menace ought not to be tolerated by decent people." There was no doubt about it—the Styx had to be moved.

Flagler was not the owner of the Styx property. It belonged to two brothers, John and Edward Bradley, who bowed to pressure and began sending out eviction notices with the intention of having the entire population gone by 1912. This much is known, but now the legend, if it is that, begins.

To celebrate the work they completed on an extremely difficult schedule, Flagler, it was said, planned a celebration for his black workers and their families in the form of an all-day carnival/circus, including a free catered buffet, games, a big top, animals, and rides. The workers rode boats over from the island to the mainland for the celebration, oblivious to what was happening behind them in the soon-to-be empty Styx.

However, the Styx was not yet completely empty. After the inhabitants were gone, white workers stealthily collected the belongings and valuables left behind by the black workers, moved it all to safety, poured gasoline on the shacks and tents, and set them on fire. The huge fire and smoke were visible on the mainland, but there was nothing anyone could do.

Or so the legend goes. While none of it has been proven to the satisfaction of many whites, the destruction of the Styx in 1912 remains believable to many black descendants. With Henry Flagler's propensity for behaving like a jerk at times and with our country's racial history, it certainly isn't difficult to imagine.

Nevertheless, Flagler went on to extend his East Coast Railroad all the way to Miami, and in his last years, he accomplished the impossible. Working four thousand men at a time, Flagler ran his railroad all the way to Key West. He was eighty-two years old when he rode the first train from Jacksonville to Key West in January 1912.

He died on January 2, 1913, with many successes and good deeds to his credit, but always with the burden of knowing the consequences of his refusal to move south for the benefit of his seriously ailing first wife, an awareness of unfair methods he and Rockefeller used when they wiped out smaller companies to form a monopoly, the knowledge of his bribing Florida legislators to pass a divorce law for his sole benefit, and, some still say, for his alleged role in the torching of Styx.

CHAPTER 6

Booker T. Washington
Gives a Speech

Scant information is available on some Florida men named William M. Holloway, W. R. Thomas, William N. Sheats, and Sam DeBose, as prominent as their names were in the 1800s. They would surely be surprised if they could know that so many years later, the name Booker T. Washington is held in high esteem and featured in history books while their names are long forgotten.

Washington was born a slave but would become the good friend of President Theodore Roosevelt, even joining the president for dinner at the White House. Educating slaves had been declared illegal, so when he was sixteen years old, Washington traveled nearly five hundred miles alone to reach a school where he believed he could get an education. Because Booker T. Washington's illiterate mother taught him to love learning, he became firmly convinced that education was the key to developing a sense of self-worth, as well as a belief in one's importance to society.

Not content only to become educated himself, Washington would evolve into a respected educator, who in time was responsible for thousands of young people eagerly following in his footsteps. In 1895, this former slave gave a speech that is considered one of the most important speeches in United States history.

In his autobiography, *Up from Slavery,* Washington stated that although he was never quite certain, he believed he was probably born in 1856, in Franklin County, Virginia, to a slave woman who worked on a tobacco farm, and a white father, who was thought by some to have been James Burroughs, the owner of the tobacco farm. But that has not been proven. His mother first named him Booker Taliaferro. After she married another slave,

Booker T. Washington

LIBRARY OF CONGRESS, PHOTO BY HARRIS & EWING

Washington Ferguson, the boy took his stepfather's first name as his last, becoming Booker Taliaferro Washington.

After the Emancipation Proclamation freed the slaves in 1865, young Washington's mother took him, his brother, John, and sister, Amanda, to Malden, West Virginia, where his stepfather had been working in a salt mine and a coal mine. The boy worked in the salt mine in the mornings and again in the evenings to help out at home, but because his mother made sure her children had time to attend school whenever it was possible, he studied in a school for African-American children during the day.

While he was at work in the mine, Booker heard a rumor that there was an open position in the home of General Lewis Ruffner, the coal mine owner. His wife, Mrs. Viola Ruffner, was looking for a houseboy, and although she had a reputation as being difficult to work for and hard to please, Booker thought he would prefer that job to working in the mines. He was hired for five dollars a month, plunged energetically into his new job, and quickly impressed Mrs. Ruffner. While he did his chores in the Ruffner home, she encouraged him to learn to read and write. She even saw to it that he attended school for an hour a day in the winter. Her trust in him continued to grow during the approximately year and a half he worked in the Ruffner home. Unlike other boys who had held his job before him, he gradually came to think of Mrs. Ruffner as one of his best friends.

Having overheard a conversation between two miners in the coal mine about the Hampton Institute, a well-known school in Virginia for former slaves, Washington made up his mind that he wanted to attend that school. He crept closer to listen to the two men talking, and when he heard one say that poor students at the school could work for their board, he made up his mind. He was going to attend the Hampton Institute. Somehow, he saved a small amount of money, which didn't get him very far by train, but the determined teen walked the remaining four hundred miles to Hampton, Virginia, where the school was located.

He eventually got there, but without having had much food, a bath, or a change of clothing, he apparently did not make a very good impression. Initially, he was neither admitted nor denied entry. However, after a time, Washington was offered and accepted a janitorial job at the school. His attitude and determination so impressed the school authorities that they soon admitted him to the school as a student. General Chapman Armstrong, the school principal, admired the young man's perseverance and intelligence and helped him in many small ways, gradually becoming an influential mentor to Washington.

After his graduation in 1878, Washington was pleased to accept a position as an instructor at Hampton Institute. Then, three years later, when General Armstrong was asked to recommend a principal for a black normal school being planned at Tuskegee, Alabama, Washington was his immediate and wholehearted choice.

However, Washington received quite a shock when he arrived at his destination in Alabama. There were no school buildings, and, in fact, he learned that no land had been purchased for the school, nor were there supplies or equipment of any kind. All that actually existed was a fund that had been set aside by a local politician for teachers' salaries. Washington's formidable job was obvious: Secure funds, build a school, hire teachers, educate. A snap.

To his surprise, Washington found that he was good at securing funding for the school. While he worked at that, he started classes for thirty students inside a church. He did not ignore standard subjects, but Washington also saw to it that subjects such as horticulture, dressmaking, brick making, carpentry, bee culture, and dairying were being taught. Some students published a newspaper on their own press, while others operated a machine shop and a tin shop.

As his reputation spread, he was befriended by men with deep pockets and generous inclinations—John D. Rockefeller, George Eastman, and Andrew Carnegie among them. But even the students pitched in, growing some of their own food and actually constructing their own beds, at the same time as they went about learning farming methods.

In 1882, Washington found time to marry Fannie Smith, his childhood sweetheart. A daughter, Portia, was born the following year, but Fannie lived only for another year after giving birth. Washington then took a second wife, Olivia Davidson, in 1885. Olivia also worked at Tuskegee and gave birth to two boys, but tragically, she died in 1889. Washington's marriage to Margaret Murray in 1893 produced no children, and his third wife would outlive him.

As the Tuskegee Institute campus grew to more than 540 acres in 1891, enrollment escalated too, to about four hundred students. A few years later, Washington opened an agricultural school, hiring George Washington Carver to head it.

Such impressive educational advances were being noticed and Washington received invitations to speak at various events and to share his principles on racial education, status, and compromises necessary for advancement. In 1893, when he was scheduled to fulfill several speaking engagements in Boston, he received an invitation to speak at an international meeting of Christian Workers in Atlanta, Georgia. He calculated that he could travel by train and be in Atlanta thirty minutes before he would be due to begin giving an address that was to last exactly five minutes. The audience of two thousand people would be composed of whites with enough clout to influence fund acquisition at Tuskegee, and that was vital. It was an honor to be invited, and it could be rewarding financially and otherwise.

Washington made the trip, arriving at his destination with seconds to spare before he was due to speak. However, his speech was well received—so well received, in fact, that it would lead to his delivering another one that is referred to as one of the most important and influential speeches in American history.

In the spring of 1895, a group of twenty-five notable, mostly white Atlanta citizens contacted Washington, asking him to accompany them to Washington, DC, to petition a congressional committee for help for the upcoming Atlanta Cotton States and International Exposition to be held in Atlanta in September. He agreed, and in spite of his misgivings about addressing members of Congress, he overcame his nervousness and received hearty congratulations afterward, and the sought-after appropriations were granted.

Back in Atlanta after their successful trip, the authorities of the exposition decided to include a separate building devoted entirely to Negro progress since the Emancipation. It was to be designed by, built by, and filled with the accomplishments of Negroes. When they decided that a black man should give the opening address on the first day of the exposition, the question of whom to ask hardly needed any discussion at all. Booker T. Washington was chosen unanimously.

The former slave accepted the invitation with gratitude and humility. In *Up from Slavery,* which he would publish in 1901, he recalled that when he was preparing to give this speech, he could not help thinking that it had only been a few years before that time that "any of the white men in the audience might have claimed me as his slave; and it was easily possible that some of my former owners might be present to hear me speak."

He knew, he said, "that this was the first time in the entire history of the Negro that a member of my race had been asked to speak from the same platform with white Southern men and women on any important national occasion. I was asked now to speak to an audience composed of the wealth and culture of the white South, the representatives of my former masters."

In his address, Washington stressed his firm belief in the value of education for Negroes. Although he extolled the value of education through reading, he also encouraged Negroes to learn to farm and to build and to produce. Over and over again, Washington said, "Cast down your bucket where you are," meaning that the vast numbers of former slaves, now freed people, must begin wherever they were—whether that was in agriculture, mechanics, or household service—and fill their "buckets" with all the knowledge they could obtain. Becoming the best farmer, builder, or home helper they could be would enable them to be economically self-supporting and therefore be of value to both races.

The speech was a sensation that night and was regarded favorably in most of the rest of the country. Granted, there were those in the black community who believed blacks needed to be more aggressive towards achieving equality immediately, and focus on obtaining a college education instead of on improving their farming or industrial skills. Nevertheless, Washington became a highly sought-after advisor and speaker.

In 1903, Florida State Superintendent of Education William N. Sheats invited Washington to speak to a group of both races at a joint meeting of the General Education Board and county superintendents of education at Gainesville. Even then, northern Florida was known to be the most "Southern" part of the state; a black man addressing an audience of white people there was sure to bring trouble. Upon learning of the discord, Washington decided to bow out, but he quickly received a telegram stating, "Come without fail. You will receive kindly and friendly welcome. Address to be given in courthouse to both races." Despite the reassurance, Washington decided against making the trip.

He also had been refusing invitations to visit Gainesville from another black man, Sam DeBose. DeBose was attempting to start an industrial school for blacks with nonexistent finances. He was convinced that with Washington's past history and spreading fame, a visit from him would be an enormous help.

At about the same time in 1902, Robert Ogden, a New York City businessman, founded the Southern Education Board, and John D. Rockefeller, the Standard Oil chief, organized the General Education Board to promote education through philanthropy. The two organizations held a joint meeting in Athens, Georgia, and agreed to allocate funds for Southern education through various community officials.

Assuming that some of those funds were going to be made available for educating black youths, DeBose convinced Sheats it was again time to ask Washington to come to Gainesville for a talk.

Having heard Washington speak, Sheats, known as "Florida's little giant of education," was convinced Washington's methods were the right ones, and that it was absolutely necessary to educate blacks to become a valued part of the workforce. He declared that he had never heard "a more noble defense of the attitude of the Southern white man towards the negro. Booker T. Washington advocates teaching the Negro how to work and how to do something and not teaching him books alone. I say he is right."

Word of Washington's upcoming visit spread all over the South, but Sheats's accepting attitude was not unanimous. Widespread muttering concerning racial purity and newspaper criticisms increased, especially following the news that President Theodore Roosevelt had hosted Washington for dinner at the White House.

Critical editorials proliferated throughout Florida newspapers, along with cartoons ridiculing President Roosevelt. The *Ocala Banner* made one common pronouncement that Southern whites must preserve "the purity of the white race . . . we owe that much to our women, to our country, to our God."

The *Palmetto News* prayerfully pronounced, "there never lived (and please God there never will) a white man so low in the social world but he was ten times better than the most respectable negro."

The volume of criticism continued to increase when it became known that Washington was scheduled to speak to white educators in a white school auditorium.

Holloway, who planned to run against Sheats for the job of state superintendent of education the following year, saw an opportunity to add many prospective voters to his side. In a display of behavior that most definitely qualified him as a jerk, he exhibited Sheats's message to DeBose confirming the invitation to Washington. He then issued a statement declaring the auditorium unavailable for a speech by Washington. Furthermore, Holloway proclaimed that he believed "social equality inconsistent with the ideas, customs and institutions of the South, and consequently inimical to her highest good and best interests, I can not sit idly by and permit so serious an infraction of her social laws as has been attempted. I therefore declare the auditorium unavailable for the use of Booker T. Washington, or any other colored person during the convention of superintendents or upon any subsequent occasion."

Insults were traded back and forth. State Senator H. H. McCreary was also the publisher and editor of the *Gainesville Sun*. He was openly opposed to Sheats's reelection as state superintendent because Sheats opposed McCreary's proposed uniform textbook bill and also a teacher certification bill. Sheats was not the only one who claimed McCreary would benefit financially from the textbook bill and that the teacher certification bill would protect incompetent teachers.

McCreary sought revenge. He printed numerous editorials that criticized Sheats, including his opinion that it was a "grave insult" to have arranged for Washington to speak before a white audience in a white school auditorium in the first place. For all to read, he printed Holloway's statement declaring the auditorium was unavailable. The number of jerks involved increased.

Sheats hastily tried to make amends, telling a reporter that Washington would "doubtlessly behave himself as approvingly to the general public as will the politest Negro waiter in a city hotel."

It was inevitable that the unpleasant discourse—including Holloway's statement of protest against social equality—published in widely available newspapers, would reach Washington in Tuskegee. True to form, he politely offered to withdraw.

At Sheats's request, Gainesville's Mayor Thomas called a meeting of a dozen Gainesville leaders to discuss the situation and the demand that Sheats be disapproved and the invitation to Washington be retracted. The tumultuous meeting had been going on for six hours when Sheats made a totally unexpected appearance, defending himself and offering that the entire mess was an attempt by Holloway to make him look bad and cause him to lose the upcoming election. The meeting ended, having accomplished nothing constructive.

Nevertheless, the leaders did agree to re-invite Washington to speak and settled on moving the event from the school to the courthouse. For unexplained reasons, Washington sent no response to Thomas, Sheats, and Holloway's first two messages, both of which guaranteed Washington a cordial reception. But Washington finally did accept their third invitation.

The public hassle caught the attention of newspapers all around the country, many of them focusing on Southern prejudice. The *Sacramento Record Union* was just one of many, which stated, "If the people of Gainesville . . . had half of Washington's manliness, politeness, and ability, they would never have been guilty of their unmannerly act."

Most, though not all, Southern papers differed. The *Houston Daily Post* hastened to inform readers that the "Florida incident does not reflect the best southern sentiment."

In Florida, comments were fairly predictable. The Jacksonville *Florida Times-Union* gave Washington credit for his accomplishments in education, while praising him for knowing "his place as a negro." As always, there were the criticisms from certain blacks, specifically that Washington and his followers at Tuskegee discouraged other blacks from aiming higher and encouraged them to be satisfied with their inferior status.

Washington was greeted enthusiastically at all his stops along the way to Gainesville and by approving crowds when he arrived. The speech was scheduled to be given in the courthouse—which was lit by electric lights and divided into white and black sections—and with sheriff deputies acting as ushers. Nothing had been overlooked.

Except perhaps the size of the crowd, which was estimated at two thousand people, all of them determined to get into the courtroom to hear Washington speak. They spilled over into the halls, and eventually out into the street. When Washington arrived at about 8 p.m., he needed a sheriff to make a path through the crowd to the courtroom, where he was introduced by Sheats.

Frequent applause interrupted his two-hour speech, in which he repeated over and over his trust in the goodness of whites and the value of blacks. He scored points with the white listeners by saying that "every man who does not produce his own living is a burden upon the pockets of the man who does work," and with his oft-repeated belief that "as one race is lifted up and made more intelligent, useful, and honest," both races become stronger.

Unmistakable enthusiasm poured from the audience at the end of Washington's speech. Many lined up to shake his hand, and he received multiple invitations to speak at other events, as well as to visit Gainesville again. Newspapers all around the country were lavish in their praise for Washington and for Gainesville for staging the event.

Ironically, most of those who made the arrangements to bring Washington to Florida were not rewarded. Sheats lost his first major election when Holloway defeated him in the Democratic primary race the next year. Returning to his previous jerk-like behavior, Holloway visited Florida's backwoods areas and passed around forty thousand copies of the Sheats letter confirming to DeBose the invitation to Washington, which had included the phrase "white school auditorium." He pointed out that by issuing an invitation to Washington, "a great man, but unfortunately . . . a negro," Sheats had "trampled underfoot the most sacred traditions which a people ever cherished."

Sheats then instigated charges of forgery related to the copies of his letter, but he lost the election by more than four thousand votes. Adding to his woes, campaign expenses left him financially drained, but he kept trying to have Holloway declared unfit for office by the State Democratic Executive Committee, hoping they would then name Sheats as their candidate. The committee did denounce Holloway, but chose another member rather than Sheats; nevertheless, that man was defeated by Holloway in the state election. It was a blow to the man once described by an executive officer in the General Education Board as having done "more than any other southerner to promote universal education."

In addition, Holloway exerted his influence as Alachua County Superintendent of Education to continue the trend of decreasing public financing of black schools, even though the taxes paid by blacks in Florida were demonstrated to be greater than the funds spent on black schools. Statistics showed that from 1895 to 1896, Florida spent $4.25 for each black child's education, while it spent $10.51 for every white child in school. Then during Holloway's Alachua County administration, the money for blacks fell to $3.37, while it increased nearly 20 percent for whites.

Unfortunately but not unexpectedly, it was a situation that Sheats was unable to change.

Booker T. Washington wasn't able to make much of a dent in the Southern thinking about race either, no matter that he had been the cause of so much excitement and even adulation when he visited Gainesville. In fact, what the celebrated visit did was give Holloway another sort of cover while he and the multitudes of jerks who thought like him went on about their business as usual for years to come.

CHAPTER 7

Guy Bradley's Killer

In 1947, Marjory Stoneman Douglas captured one sentiment in particular better than anyone has before or since. "There are no other Everglades in the world," she said in her book, *The Everglades: River of Grass.*

"Unique" is a word often applied to the thousands of square miles of low, flat sawgrass marshes, slanted just enough that water passes over them. Although the Everglades are home to countless species of animals on the land and fish in the water, most noticeable to humans would be the vast numbers of resident birds: pelicans, crows, snowy egrets, grackles, roseate spoonbills, mockingbirds, anhinghas, limpkins, woodpeckers, herons, vultures, and more.

Like the rest of our country, two hundred years ago, all of Florida was home to nearly infinite numbers and species of birds. There were birds paddling in the water, singing in the trees, and soaring in the sky, as they have been since the beginning of time. But in the late 1800s, when people looked up, they finally realized that something had changed. There were fewer birds, there were fewer avian species, and it was becoming apparent that unregulated hunting was decimating the native species of Florida birds. Animals, too, were being hunted and killed by the millions for their skins, but the state of affairs was even more precarious for birds. The situation was so dire that birds coming to Florida seeking refuge from more northern regions had been driven farther and farther south into the Everglades. The rather absurd reason for the dilemma was a ridiculous fashion trend: Decorating ladies' hats with feathers had become the latest rage. Unfortunately, this trend proved to be particularly disastrous. In 1886, it was estimated that five million birds were being killed each year to supply milliners.

In those days, no lady left home without a hat on her head, and the most stylish women wore hats with feathers. Chiefly desired were hats decorated with aigrettes, the long and curved plumes of egrets and herons. However, feathers of any kind were better than none at all, and feathers obtained from birds in the breeding season were the most desirable. In fact, it was not uncommon to see hats adorned with whole bodies of dead birds—having made a trip to the taxidermist first, to be sure.

In addition, it wasn't only bird populations that were being decimated. The hides and meat of deer and the skins of alligators were in demand too. Furthermore, tourists seated on boats plying the rivers of south Florida would shoot for mere sport at anything that moved, leaving the corpse where it fell.

But it was by hunting and killing birds that the most money could be made. One French taxidermist, M. Le Chevelier, reported that at home in Paris, he could get fifty cents for a pelican skin, twenty-five cents for terns, ten dollars for a great white heron, and twenty-five dollars for a flamingo, because the last two were scarce even then. When New York milliners were willing to pay thousands of dollars for a single shipment of plumes, it is easy to understand why many hunters would willingly spend uncomfortable weeks and months in the steaming jungles, shooting birds.

One of those hunters was Walter Smith, originally from New Bern, North Carolina, a toughened veteran of the Civil War. He was eighteen years old when he enlisted, then remained with the Confederate force for the four years that the war lasted, all the while honing his abilities as a sharpshooter and a scout. He spent the last part of his enlistment in a hospital, blind in one eye from a powder burn and missing part of a bone in his left arm after a bullet had done its work.

The war ended, but Smith's hair-raising experiences didn't. At loose ends because he had no more family in North Carolina, and since he was always attracted to the sea, he decided to sign on for work on a boat. One day, the boat encountered a monstrous storm just off the Carolina coast. Smith and the rest of the crew lost control and were hurled into the sea. A strong swimmer, he was able to reach shore before he lost consciousness, and remained lying on the sand until he was rescued by a family who lived on a nearby island. Smith remained with them for a few years, then made his way farther south, where he married, bought a schooner, and continued on to Georgia. Eventually he moved on to Florida, all the way to the Palm Beach area. It was there he met the Bradley family.

Edwin and Lydia Bradley, along with their sons, Louis and Guy, and daughter, Flora, had moved from Chicago to the Lake Worth region. The United States Life Saving Service had just opened five houses along the bleak, uninhabited southern east coast of Florida to provide a place of refuge with water and food for shipwrecked sailors. Edwin gratefully accepted the government job as keeper of the Fort Lauderdale House of Refuge. The dependable salary would make the lonely life a worthwhile sacrifice for the family.

The salary, however, did not make up for the devastating health problems that afflicted the family that first winter. Louis was first to suffer with persistent fatigue, puffiness, and poor coloring. When he began to recover, Guy became ill, and his undiagnosed illness dragged on and on, continuing to plague him for several years. But the worst was Flora, who died in the spring, leaving the whole family heartbroken.

In time, two more daughters, Rose and Maggie, were born to the Bradleys. As the boys grew, they made their contributions to support the family, by hunting, fishing, farming, and—as the result of their mother's influence—in music. Lydia, a trained musician, taught the children to play various instruments and then joined with them to form the Hypoluxo String Band. The family band played at most of the area dances for some time.

Edwin, who briefly delivered mail, turned to writing for a local newspaper before he was named to be the superintendent of schools for Dade County. He continued both jobs while he farmed and sold fertilizer on the side. Maintaining a family in southern Florida was not easy.

Guy and Louis found that one of the few reliable ways they could make any money in south Florida was by plume hunting. When they were young, the boys often had joined their friends in plume hunting expeditions. It was a way to make small amounts of money that was more fun than digging sweet potatoes or other jobs for their father. As adults, they continued to take advantage of any opportunity to hunt and shoot birds for their feathers.

By the time he was twenty-two years old, Guy was being called Captain Bradley, having been hired to deliver mail in the family boat, covering a distance of about twenty miles. He then moved on to take charge of the boat belonging to an acquaintance, Albert Robert, the land agent for Henry Flagler. His father moved on, too, resigning from his position as superintendent of schools to become the assistant superintendent of Flagler's Florida Coast Line Canal and Transportation Company. The company was digging up a channel for a canal that would become part of the Intracoastal Waterway.

As Flagler's endeavors expanded and moved on, it was apparent that lands at the tip of Florida would need to be developed. Edwin Bradley accepted the position as agent for the Model Land Company in the Cape Sable area. He hoped returning his family to life in the wilderness would be offset by the financial gains he was convinced would materialize as a result of Flagler's investing in the region. It would most certainly be an exciting opportunity to take advantage of financially if Flagler ended his railroad at Cape Sable as was rumored.

Included in Edwin's agreement with the Model Land Company, Guy and Louis each received a quarter of a mile of land along Florida Bay. Life for the Bradley family was definitely improving. In 1899, Guy married Sophronia "Fronie" Vickers, a young widow from Key West; one year later their son, Morrell, was born.

The town where the Bradleys settled in 1898 was named Flamingo, a reference to the brilliant pink birds that made their home in the area before scant civilization arrived, though the birds had already moved on. The family was surprised to find their old neighbors, the Walter Smith family, living in Flamingo when they moved there. In fact, Smith was the town postmaster.

Smith thought that since his oldest son, Tommy, was only ten and that it was good to have help with large bird shoots, the sons of his old neighbors might be interested in accompanying him on his hunts. Louis and Guy most surely were interested in an easy way to add to their incomes, although it was about this time that they were beginning to hear some disturbing criticisms about plume hunting.

Kirk Monroe and his wife, Mary Barr Monroe, old friends from the Lake Worth area, had kept in touch with the Bradleys and visited with them occasionally. Kirk, the founding vice president of the Florida Audubon Society, was gaining fame as a writer for *Scribner's Magazine* and *Harper's Weekly*. Kirk and Mary were both well educated and had become familiar with leaders of the developing conservation movement during visits to New York City several times a year. In fact, Mary had a reputation for snatching feathered hats right off the heads of women she passed in the street. News of the brand-new Audubon Society, of Theodore Roosevelt's work in protecting wildlife, and of the establishment of the Sierra Club were some of the conservation topics the Monroes shared with the Bradley family. Guy, especially, thought long and hard about what he was hearing, and gradually began to change his mind about plume hunting.

On May 28, 1901, under pressure from State Senator W. Hunt Harris, Florida passed Chapter 4357, "An Act for the Protection of Birds and Their Nests and Eggs, and Prescribing a Penalty for any Violation Thereof." Although it omitted any provision for hiring a warden to enforce the new law, money for that was provided by a successful wildlife painter, Abbott Thayer. When Kirk Monroe's advice was sought about someone to fill the job, he did not hesitate to recommend his old friend, Guy Bradley, who was happy to accept.

Guy felt proud to be sworn in as game warden and as deputy sheriff. Having been a plume hunter himself in the past, he was

Guy Bradley wearing his deputy badge
HISTORYMIAMI

well suited for the job. He knew the ways of hunters as well as anyone, and he was familiar with the confusing region around the Ten Thousand Islands, where plume hunters could easily evade pursuit.

He knew something else: It wasn't going to be easy. It was an enormous area that he would be responsible for patrolling. He would be away from his young family much of the time and living in the most primitive conditions. Along with his other duties, he was expected to try to find out the names of the firms in the cities that were dealing in illegal plumes, and also to submit a monthly report. Moreover, there would always be the element of danger in confronting men with guns, some of them troublemakers not in the best of moods.

In addition, the neighborhood troublemaker, Walter Smith, was antagonizing many of the settlers in Flamingo. Guy's brother-in-law, Bill Burton, and sister, Maggie, had won a legal dispute with Smith over the boundary line between their property and Smith's. The survey determined the Burtons were correct, but the surveyor was Guy Bradley, which further fed the fire of bad feelings.

Smith was also involved in a squabble with other neighbors over securing a teacher and a schoolhouse for the town. The schoolhouse was not a problem. They had already built a single-room building to be used as a schoolhouse, or for church or other meetings. But securing a teacher caused a major dispute. Smith and another town leader, Steve Roberts, were each certain they knew who was best for the job, and neither would back down. Underlying the dispute was the problem that both men felt entitled to be considered the town's boss. Smith came out on top in this to-do, but the bitterness with his neighbors escalated.

Meanwhile, things were beginning to look up for the conservationists. On March 14, 1903, President Teddy Roosevelt signed an executive order creating the nation's first wildlife refuge, the Pelican Island Reservation on Florida's central east coast. Shortly after that, the Audubon Society provided Guy with a twenty-three-foot power craft to replace his small sailboat, as the latter was difficult to maneuver when there was no wind.

Guy and Fronie were expecting their second baby, and they decided it would be best to move to Key West where, if she needed help during Guy's absences, she could call her best friend, who lived nearby.

The Bradley family experienced good news and bad news that fall. Edwin learned that Henry Flagler was heading his railroad to Key West rather than Cape Sable, which made the family land investments almost worthless. But the good news was that on November 8, 1903, Ellis Bradley, Guy and Fronie's second son, was born.

Even so, the difficulties with Walter Smith not only continued but escalated. Guy had to make three arrests for shooting birds illegally—one of the elder Captain Smith and two of Tom Smith, Walter's oldest boy. Tom was seventeen years old—old enough to know he had to obey the law, Guy felt, and he believed the boy would continue to defy it if he were lenient with the teenager.

Guy felt he had no choice in whether to enforce the law—even after the second arrest, when Walter Smith snarled, "You ever arrest one of my boys again, I'll kill you."

And Smith could not have been pleased when on March 22, 1905, the Florida secretary of state notified Guy that he was officially the "Fish and Game Warden in and for Monroe County."

Not long after Guy's official appointment, the Smith family— Walter, his wife, Rebecca, and their five children—were relaxing at home one evening when suddenly gunshots flew though the air into their thin-walled home. Smith shouted at his family to stay down on the floor while shots continued to fly, then stopped as suddenly as they had started. Smith cautiously made his way to the door to see what he could see, but it was dark, and there was no one in sight.

He was convinced the perpetrator had to be his adversary, Steve Roberts, and his gang. In Smith's mind, Guy Bradley was included in that gang. Smith quickly boarded his boat and took off for Key West. He knew exactly where to go to buy a powerful rifle, a Winchester .38. Smith planned to be ready—really ready—for the next time.

Some months later, Guy heard shots shatter the quiet morning of July 8, 1905. Looking out his front door, across the bay, he recognized the schooner that was anchored near Oyster Keys, about two miles away. He knew it was Smith's boat and knew what he had to do. His brother, Louis, and brother-in-law, Bill, who had helped him in the past, were both out of town, but Guy had no choice: It was his duty to investigate. To make matters worse, the powerboat needed repair and was unusable. With no wind, the sailboat was useless. He had to row a dinghy a long, tiresome way, but he felt he must do it.

Smith watched Guy rowing towards him, all the while keeping an eye on two of his sons, Tom and Danny. Because of the low tide, he couldn't move his schooner out of the mud until the tide changed. He had allowed the boys to leave the boat so they could fire into the island rookery from where they were wading in the shallow water.

Smith fired one shot into the air, a prearranged signal for his boys to stop shooting birds and get back to the boat. Defying their father and the warden, the boys fired their guns once again before they climbed aboard with their latest haul of two cormorants.

Without other eyewitnesses, only Smith's version of the events that happened next was available.

He later said that Guy asked for his son, Tom, and in answer to Smith's demand for a warrant, Guy had replied he didn't need one, since he had seen the boys shoot into the rookery and they had dead birds in their possession.

Smith said he then accused Guy of being one of the ones who had fired into his house and that if he wanted Tom, he would have to come aboard the Smith boat and get him. He said they had a few more exchanges and Guy cursed at him and fired at him with his pistol, but missed. Smith returned the fire with his rifle, he said, and Guy dropped down on his dinghy, which drifted away.

When high tide rolled in, Smith headed home.

Meanwhile, Fronie was terrified. She heard the gunshot and recognized Smith's boat in the distance before it sailed away. She was used to the fact that Guy often had to be away at night, but Oyster Bay was within sight of their home. She thought he should have been home by then. She wondered what else had happened. It would be a long, fretful day—and night.

Then, after a sleepless night, she could stand to wait no longer. She called on the Roberts family for help. They came at once, and Gene Roberts headed out into the bay where he finally came upon Guy's boat, his dead body, and his unfired revolver.

Smith, in the meantime, informed his family he was leaving for Key West to give himself up. "I've killed Guy Bradley," he said.

When he confessed to the shooting, the sheriff took him into custody and notified State Senator W. Hunt Harris, the newly appointed prosecuting attorney, who recommended Smith be held while evidence was collected. That was when Senator W. Hunt Harris did something that propelled him into the category of Florida jerks—he took on the job of defense attorney for the prime jerk in the case, Walter Smith, at the preliminary hearing. Hunt, the man who a week before had been the prosecuting attorney, was now the defense attorney.

The grand jury was not scheduled to hold a hearing on the case until November and in fact did not meet until December, which gave Senator Harris plenty of time to do his new job. Guy Bradley had been defending an environmental law that was unpopular in Monroe County, and so residents felt little sympathy for anyone whose job it was to enforce it. On the other hand, it never hurt for elected officials to demonstrate their shared feelings with their constituents.

In addition, Smith had done an excellent job of making valuable connections among the powerful in Key West. The connections would enable him to grease whatever palms needed it. It didn't matter that the bullets were all still in Guy's pistol or that the position of its firing pin showed it hadn't been fired. Smith was freed.

Devastated members of the Audubon Society started a fund for the family of the man who gave his life for the protection of birds. The fund's ongoing donations allowed Fronie to buy a home in Key West and live fairly comfortably with her sons.

The killing of birds went on, however, and in fact, two more wardens were murdered as a result of the plume trade. It was not until World War II that the slowly dying plume trade finally ended.

Smith moved his family to a farm in Pompano, his past forgotten. When he died in 1935, his obituary mentioned his service in the Confederate Army, but nothing about his murder of Guy Bradley. Tom, his son, joined the police force in Pompano.

The Audubon Society erected a monument to honor their fallen deputy with a plaque that read:

Guy M. Bradley
1870–1905
Faithful Unto Death,
Game Warden of Monroe
County. He Gave His Life for
The Cause to Which He Was
Pledged.

CHAPTER 8

Edgar J. Watson, Killing Machine

If ever a Florida citizen qualified to be branded as a jerk, Edgar J. Watson surely is it. Some of the stories that are told about him may not be true, but enough of them have been proven to put him near the top of the list of the worst of the worst. He most certainly started his moral decline earlier than the others—at the tender age of nine if one tale about him is true.

Watson was born on November 11, 1855, in South Carolina, to Ellen Catherine and Lige Watson. Lige, a prison warden with a reputation for cruelty toward both his wards and his family, was nicknamed "Ring Eye" for a scar he carried around one eye, the result of a circular knife wound acquired in a fight.

Apparently he passed his cruelty gene on to his son. The boy was nine years old when he supposedly killed a black man who had been about to report some of Edgar's bad behavior to his father.

Finally, Ellen Catherine, the recipient of much of her husband's cruelty, had enough. She took Edgar and his sister, Minnie, and escaped to safety with relatives living near Lake City, Florida.

Edgar grew into a tall, good-looking, blue-eyed, red-haired and red-bearded young man, well dressed and well mannered. He married for the first of what would eventually be three times and began what it seemed would be a normal life. He rented and worked a farm for a while, but his raging genes came to the forefront again. During a drunken tavern fight, he killed a cousin, badly damaged his own kneecap, and lost the farm.

In another tavern fight before he and his wife moved out of Florida, he reportedly killed three more men. It was a good time to pull up stakes.

With his family, he headed for Indian Territory, and it was there that he became acquainted with the notorious Belle Starr, also known as the Bandit Queen. Seeking some property to farm,

Edgar J. Watson

ALVIN M. LEDERER

the Watsons paid her cash in advance to lease a parcel of her land. Later, as they became better acquainted, Mrs. Watson made the mistake of confiding to Belle Starr that her husband was wanted for murder in Florida.

Having been previously warned by the Cherokee tribal council that she would be expelled from her lands if there were any serious trouble, Belle confronted Watson, demanding that he clear off her land. At first he refused, but the bickering escalated, and it was at the same time that accusations of horse thievery were being leveled at him too. Faced with Belle's threats of reporting him to the Florida authorities and her insistence that he accept the money he had paid her for the farm rental, Watson decided that leaving the territory appeared to be the best option.

Then in 1889, two days before Belle's forty-first birthday, she was riding home after shopping and visiting some neighbors in Eufaula, Oklahoma. She was riding her horse along a trail not far from Watson's cabin when a shotgun blast seemed to come from nowhere. The force knocked her off her horse, and as she was struggling to get to her feet, another shot struck her in the shoulder. When another shot hit her face, Belle Starr was dead. Her horse bolted and galloped home without her.

Tracks of footprints appearing to be in Watson's shoe size were detected leading from the murder scene toward his cabin, but they stopped short of his place. Some neighbors claimed they heard shots, but no one had actually seen anything.

Although Watson was charged with the murder, the distinguished attorney he hired presented an impressive case insisting all the evidence against him was circumstantial. Watson was acquitted, and wisely fled the Indian Territory. Several other people were suspected of the murder, including Belle's son, with whom she had been having an ongoing and bitter feud, but without actual witnesses the case was never solved. However, Watson lost no time in getting far away from the fracas—all the way to Oregon.

Little is known of the circumstances, but according to sketchy reports, his wife died, and he married again, fathered four children, and allegedly murdered again too, although the records are spotty, conflicted, and enhanced with rumors and the shaky recollections of old-timers.

He left that family behind when he returned to Florida in 1891. In Arcadia for a short time, he promptly got himself involved in another unpleasantness in a tavern with a thug named Quinn Bass. Watson solved this brawl with his Smith & Wesson revolver, making him responsible for one more dead body.

He then made another hasty move, this time to the Ten Thousand Islands, where he settled in and started to work the cane fields. In 1892, he built a substantial two-story white house on an Indian mound of sand and shells. With a third-story attic and a porch with a sweeping view of the river, Watson's was the largest home in the islands.

The Ten Thousand Islands is a remote area where clusters of mangroves form thousands of tiny islands. In the late 1800s, the area attracted the dregs of society—murderers and all kinds of other undesirables who were running from the law. Luck was with Watson when the owner of a forty-acre island property, approximately twenty miles south of Chokoloskee, called Chatham Bend, was gunned down by police. The victim's widow sold Chatham Bend to him for $250, and Watson lost no time turning it into a flourishing enterprise.

He grew sugar cane, papayas, vegetables, and horse bananas. Rather than ship the sugar cane, he turned it into cane syrup and transported tons of it in metal containers. He also did well selling cords of buttonwood, which settlers used for firewood and for making charcoal. Business was so good that he bought the *Veatlis,* an old, seventy-two-foot schooner, to haul his products on regular runs all the way to Key West and Tampa.

While he made those runs, he usually scouted for hired help to work on his farm, favoring mostly vagabonds or migrants or men with no families, and occasionally women who were single or widowed. That way, most of his workers had no one to inquire after them if something happened to them. Neighbors noticed that he would bring his new workers back to the farm on his schooner, but in time the people who lived there began to realize that they never saw any of the workers leave. Gradually, locals became convinced that Watson had devised his own method of obtaining a source of cheap labor. He would never have to pay them—on payday he killed them instead. He would either bury them among the alligator-infested mangroves or toss them overboard into the Gulf of Mexico. How many had there been? Only Watson knew.

The first big mess that Watson got into that his neighbors knew about happened in Key West, where he had gone for a land auction. While there, he ran into Adolphus Santini, a seafaring Corsican and the largest landowner in Chokoloskee. When Santini outbid Watson for a piece of land, they got into an argument that escalated into a real brawl. In a fury, Watson cut Santini's throat and most likely would have killed him had not bystanders forcibly taken the knife from Watson and calmed things down. Santini survived, but Watson had to pay nine hundred dollars to settle the matter out of court, a small price for nearly taking a man's life.

Not long after that incident, Watson paid for a land parcel on nearby Lost Man's River. Unfortunately, a man named Tucker was squatting on the parcel and refused to leave. Watson notified him by letter that he had to vacate and, in return, received a less than mannerly letter from Tucker refusing to leave. A few days later, Tucker paid for that mistake when he and one of his nephews were murdered. Watson was suspected, but never formally accused.

Nevertheless, Watson considered that it might be a good idea to escape the pointing fingers, so he traveled north again for a time. He tried farming in North Carolina for a while, but it wasn't long before he got himself into another saloon brawl that ended with two men dead and fingers again pointed at him. According to observers, he paid a hefty sum to get out of that one successfully before he headed back to Chatham Bend.

Like most of the other men who lived in the Ten Thousand Islands in those days, Watson made some of his money as a plume hunter and an alligator skinner, but he was chiefly a distributor of agricultural products and syrup from his sugar cane. One neighbor said his syrup, called Island Pride, was thick as honey with an indescribably delicious taste.

Not only did Watson own the largest house on the island, he built a mill, which he outfitted to make the syrup and seal it in square tin containers. He also had a warehouse constructed next to the mill to store his products, as well as docks on the river for his two schooners and a smaller gasoline-powered launch.

He seemed to be living the good life, but still, the rumors never ceased, and apparently, his shadowy life did not either. He must have known that he was being called "Bloody Ed" and "Emperor Watson" behind his back, but it didn't appear to bother him.

There were lighter moments, however, depending on who was telling the story. Once, after a long visit to a saloon in Tampa, Watson stopped at a hardware store on an errand and overheard one of the store workers telling a tale concerning a dancing school. Watson whipped out a pistol from his belt and shot at the feet of the other man, saying, "Well, let's see how nice you can dance." There was no real harm done, but he spent the night in jail for that one.

Another escapade cost him dearly. On a brief trip north to Lake City, Watson married his third wife. A good friend of the new wife had died recently and willed some silver and a piano to her. However, the surviving widower, Sam Toland, made the mistake of refusing to turn the piano and silver over to Watson's bride, arousing the ire of the bridegroom, who, as might be expected by this time, shot Toland. Watson was charged with murder and tried in Jacksonville, but was acquitted for lack of evidence. For once, he listened and followed a friend's advice when he was told, "Get back to the Ten Thousand Islands as fast as you can—and stay there."

Despite his history, Watson could get along with people when he wanted to. The postmaster and owner of the general store, Charles S. Smallwood, and his wife, Mamie, both liked Watson. They too were originally from South Carolina, and they liked talking with him and reminiscing about their home state. They also counted him as one of their best customers, a man who always paid his bills promptly and never gave them a lick of trouble. Watson even bragged to Smallwood that he had killed Belle Starr but said he wasn't looking for any more trouble. The Smallwoods and the Watsons dined together fairly often without ever having any difficulties. Although there were a few other people in Chokoloskee who admitted to liking Watson, they were, to be sure, in the minority with their opinions.

However, once when a deputy sheriff from Monroe County came to investigate rumors concerning the disappearance of his workers, Watson disarmed the sheriff and forced him to work cutting sugar cane in his fields before he allowed the deputy to leave, with menacing instructions to stay out of Chatham Bend.

Through his various shady connections, Watson had provided several fugitives from justice with living accommodations on his property. Among them were Herbert "Duchy" Melvin, who had been sentenced to hang for killing a Key West policeman but through legal finagling had had his sentence reduced to one year. Through the convict-lease system, he was employed by the Key West Fire Department, which provided an opportunity to organize some of his cohorts into a gang specializing in robbery and arson. Melvin had already spent time in prison before arriving at Chatham Bend. Not much was known about another man, Leslie Cox—an escaped convict from Madison County before he joined the group at Watson's property—but it was suspected that he might have been a partner of Watson's in the past. Also in the group were Frank Waller, a man no one seems to know much about; Hannah Smith, a three-hundred-pound woman who was an alligator hunter; and a young black man named Sip Linsy.

With a cast like that, people who lived in the area could not have been surprised when trouble broke out at Chatham's Bend. The young black man, Linsy, escaped from the group, ran, and made his way through the Florida jungle into town, where he fearfully spilled his story to some farmers and fishermen. He claimed that while Watson was on a trip, Cox confided that he had been hired to kill Smith, Waller, and Linsy, but promised Linsy that if he helped with the murders, Cox would let him go, providing he left the island. Cox didn't say for sure who hired him, but Linsy was certain it must have been Watson. Linsy was so terrified that he helped kill Smith and Waller, but he hadn't left yet when Watson and Melvin returned. He helped Cox kill Melvin and throw his body in the creek. Then Cox disappeared.

Later, some fishermen were heading up the creek on their way to Possum Creek to do some clamming when they saw a foot sticking up out of the water near Watson's property. They pulled over next to it, and after a struggle, managed to pull a very large woman's body from the water. They were horrified to see the woman had been cut opened and stuffed with two hundred pounds of pig iron weights to make her sink and that the corpse was three-hundred-pound Hannah Smith. The fisherman and his friends dragged Smith out of the muck and quietly buried her.

The nearest officers of the law were in Key West, Tampa, or Fort Myers, more than a day away, so there was no discussion about notifying anyone. The citizens in the Ten Thousand Islands made their own laws and enforced them as they saw fit.

It so happened that a short time later, the great hurricane of 1910 hurtled through Monroe County, but fortunately it didn't cause much damage as it went right on past. Watson had gone to Fort Myers to try to convince Sheriff Frank Tippins to accompany him and arrest Cox, but the weather had forced him to seek shelter.

Consequently, he was gone from the area when a group of men—farmers, fishermen, and merchants—talked it over and decided to form a posse.

There had been ugly rumors before, but this was different. Linsy had been so obviously devastated and terrified to have been completely at the mercy of someone who was planning to murder him. He was someone who had been there, who had seen the killings. The men felt this could not be ignored.

Knowing that Watson wasn't home, the men made their way to his place and found what they didn't want to find: human bones and skulls. Later, the final count would come to more than fifty.

In the meantime, Watson continued on his way back home as soon as the weather settled sufficiently. He stopped at Smallwood's store to buy shotgun shells, unaware that the shells had not yet dried out from the hurricane's deluge that had soaked almost everything. Before he left the store, he confided to Smallwood that he was going to kill Cox himself.

The following day, October 24, 1910, one week after the hurricane, was Watson's regular day to lay in supplies at the Smallwood Trading Post. It was part of his weekly routine, and everyone, including the neighbors, knew that. Fortified with whiskey, the posse waited at Smallwood's landing, listening for the sound of Watson's boat engine.

Watson's wife, who had been frightened and expected the worst, was staying in the Smallwood house with Mrs. Smallwood. When the crowd began to gather at the landing by the store, Smallwood, too, expected nothing good was going to happen that day. He went up to his house to try to allay the women's fears, and hoping to avoid being directly involved in the sad ruckus that he knew was coming.

Watson finally arrived, pulled his boat up onto the sand, picked up his shotgun from the bottom of his boat, and called out that he had killed Cox and dumped him in the swamp. When the men asked what proof he had, he showed them all that was left of Cox—his hat. It had a bullet hole in it, from the bullet that had killed Cox, Watson said.

Because Smallwood had already told the men that the shells he had sold to Watson were wet and useless, they didn't believe Watson's tale. They would need more proof, they told him. He needed to give them his gun, they said. With that, he lifted his gun, saying, "I'll give you my gun." He aimed it at the posse and pulled the trigger, only to hear it click harmlessly for a few seconds before the ear-shattering blast of the posse's guns riddled his body and he dropped.

No one would ever know whose gun it was that did the job. More than thirty-three bullets would later be found in his body.

Inside the Smallwood house, Mrs. Watson said, "My God, they have killed Mr. Watson!"

The men quietly passed a bottle of whiskey around again before they tied the bloody body by the neck to the stern of a boat and dragged it through the water to Rabbit Key. They would later say they had chosen to move the body that way to keep from getting blood all over their boat. They buried Watson without a casket of any kind, but his widow's family in Fort Myers eventually had the body recovered and returned there. They reburied it in the Fort Myers Cemetery with a stone marked simply, "Watson."

Cox was never caught and never heard from again. Only Linsy was detained for his part in the murders of Smith, Waller, and Melvin, but his detailed explanation of the events was so convincing that charges against him were dismissed. The sheriff even gave him some money, clothes, and a train ticket to his home in Georgia.

Tragic events persisted when an unnamed woman who lived in Watson's home for a time was said to have gone berserk. She set fire to all the trees on the property except one poinciana tree, which still survives. The property is now a part of the Everglades National Park, but the house burned to the ground in the 1940s.

Smallwood's store remains open as a museum and was placed on the National Register of Historic Places in 1974. It is currently being operated by Ted Smallwood's granddaughter.

Edgar Watson has been memorialized in three novels by Peter Matthiessen, based mostly on oral histories and painstaking investigation of actual records. Although Matthieson's novels are excellent award-winning literary works, it must be remembered they are novels and some of the information that is found in them is either what has become legend or is the award-winning product of the mind of a brilliant novelist.

Nevertheless, the final estimate of the number of humans killed by Watson is said to be fifty-seven, earning him a prominent place among the jerks in Florida history.

CHAPTER 9

The Divisive Governor Catts

People are seldom all good or all bad. Jerks don't usually behave like jerks all the time, but occasionally their bad behavior is so obnoxious, it's hard to remember the other times. When writing about Florida Governor Sidney Catts, historian Warren Jennings offered his opinion that "a more disruptive and divisive personality has seldom appeared on the political scene of any state."

In 1920, Governor Catts wrote the following memorable letter to the editor of the *Palm Beach Post*:

> *Dear Sir:*
>
> *I received a copy of your Palm Beach Post with your page and a half of vituperations and bitterness against me. . . . Now I have got to speak plainly to you. . . . If you print one more page in your paper like this last one . . . I will go to West Palm Beach, Florida, with my double-barrel shotgun loaded with buckshot and I will have a final settlement with you. You say your printer's ink is worth ten cents a drop, but I say 14 buckshots in each gun barrel with a man who will pull the trigger weighs one thousand pounds each. . . . This is a last warning and all that I have to say.*
>
> *Yours very truly, Sidney J. Catts*

It is hard to believe the writer of this letter was an elected politician who pushed for reforms in prisons and in the treatment of the mentally ill, endorsed women's suffrage, and worked for bank guarantees, better schools, and a reserve fund to insure bank deposits against the loss of funds. He didn't succeed in many of his efforts; nevertheless, he did try.

Sidney Catts was born in rural Pleasant Hill, Alabama, in 1863, into a family that owned and operated a successful plantation. Following his private school education, Catts earned a law degree at Cumberland School of Law in Lebanon, Tennessee, and then practiced as an attorney for three years. After his father's death, he maintained his law practice while supervising work on the family plantation for his mother.

Catts's attendance at a religious revival led to his personal conversion from the law to religion. Never lacking in self-assurance, he abandoned the legal profession, and in 1886 he accepted assignment as pastor of several parishes in Alabama near his home, despite the fact that he lacked any formal theological education.

It was a big year for Catts, for in addition to changing professions, he met and fell in love with Alice May Campbell, who had been planning to work as a teacher at Pleasant Hill. She dropped her plans to teach when they married and started to raise their family, but the young couple quickly learned how difficult that could be on a rural parson's salary.

When the Baptist church in Tuskegee asked him to be their pastor, Catts accepted eagerly. It sounded promising, considering the town's reputation as a prominent center for black education. Booker T. Washington was becoming well known as head of the Tuskegee Institute. However, even in that location, Catts maintained his lifelong belief in white supremacy. His sermons reflected his racial intolerance, hatred for Catholicism, and belief in the necessity of Prohibition. At first he seemed to fit in well with his rural parishioners, but difficulties resulting from his arrogance and fits of temper, plus the low pay, soon wore on him.

Increasingly discouraged, he resigned in 1901 to return to one of his former pastorates at Fort Deposit, Alabama, where he also dabbled in community affairs and politics. One unsuccessful try for a political office, combined with dwindling finances and a mercurial temper, ended his time as pastor at Fort Deposit.

He moved his growing family, which eventually included eight children, back to the plantation at Pleasant Hill again, where he preached part-time while he farmed. An old friend who had moved over the border to Florida convinced Catts to accept a pastorate in nearby DeFuniak Springs. It turned out to be a good change for him.

To augment with his pastor's salary, Catts began to sell insurance, a job that required much travel around the rural countryside. Through frequent meetings with ordinary people, Catts developed an intense interest in public affairs. Never one to doubt his self-worth, he began to mull over the idea of running for governor. The more he saw of the countryside, the more the idea appealed to him, especially when he considered how successfully he was developing a dynamic style of public speaking. He knew it would be as much of an asset in politics as it was in the pulpit.

It must have been difficult to maintain ties with his close-knit family, but to his credit he managed to do it. Hoping to gain support in the Democratic primary race for governor, he was busy pulling political strings in Jacksonville when his son Walter became seriously ill in Birmingham, Alabama, where was living with an older brother. Walter suffered for a long time with a chronic kidney problem, but this time he was not expected to live. Catts, so broke he had to borrow money for the train fare to Birmingham, arrived there shortly before Walter died. The family was devastated, but Catts quickly rebounded and wasted no time in resuming his gubernatorial campaign.

Also in the governor's race was William Knott, state comptroller, former state treasurer, and loyal Democrat who was considered a shoo-in by most of his party. Frederick Hudson, a Miami attorney, state senator from Miami, and ex-president of the Senate, was thought to be a possibility by others. Ion L. Farris, state senator from Jacksonville and former speaker of the house, was hopeful but a not very confident favorite of organized labor. From St. Petersburg, F. A. Wood, a retired banker and onetime House member, was also running.

In the beginning, the candidacy of the former preacher/insurance salesman was not taken seriously. In truth, Catts's run for office was at first considered a joke in Democratic political circles, but unbeknownst to them, he had some secret weapons in his arsenal. He always connected with the "little people," the "Crackers" (Floridians whose roots go back several generations), who were many and who were generally ignored by professional politicians. Catts made a point of listening to them and took pains to make sure they knew he was the only one listening to them. More importantly, he catered to the religious fundamentalism and anti-Catholic sentiment that prevailed in the rural areas all over the South.

A new semisecret organization, the Guardians of Liberty, with a membership in the hundreds of thousands, including prominent political and military men, was working to defeat Catholic politicians in the South. One well-known writer at the time, Charles P. Sweeney, wrote that he believed secret fraternal organizations and bigotry went hand in hand. He particularly cited the Guardians of Liberty, the Masons, the Knights of Pythias, the Odd Fellows, the American Mechanics, the Junior Order American Mechanics, the Woodmen of the World, the True Americans, the Sons and Daughters of Washington, and the Ku Klux Klan.

In the past, Catts had openly claimed to be a member of the Masons, the Guardians of Liberty, the Woodmen of the World, the Knights of Pythias, and the Junior Order American Mechanics. In addition, Catts was a member of the Baptist Church, Florida's most prominent denomination and the most anti-Catholic. Unexpectedly, his connection to the secret groups led to a serious difficulty for his candidacy.

In an effort to promote I. L. Farris for the governorship, J. M. Barrs, a Jacksonville attorney, drew up a resolution aimed at preventing secret political club members from being involved in Democratic primary elections. He had R. B. Sturkie, chairman of the Resolutions Committee, introduce it. The adoption of the "Sturkie Resolution" by the Executive Committee convinced Catts his effort at capturing the governorship was over. However, with help from friends and objections from others who pronounced the Sturkie Resolution an assault on the freedom of speech and of religion, the committee met again and removed the objectionable parts of the resolution. Catts was back in the running.

Another major influence on public opinion was Thomas E. Watson, a prominent Georgia writer whose *Jeffersonian Magazine* was widely read and subscribed to in Florida. His anti-Catholic rants were matched by those in another magazine, the *Menace,* which was published weekly in Missouri by Billy Parker, an aggressive young preacher who came from Pennsylvania to attract crowds on Florida street corners with his anti-Catholic speeches.

In one of Catts's more memorable efforts at speaking to the people, he informed his listeners that less than a fifth of Florida's population was Catholic, but that they held two-thirds of all public offices—both obviously inaccurate statements. He delighted in bragging that he was so offensive to Catholics that many of them wanted to kill "Old Catts," proudly adding that he had tried so hard to resist the call to enter the governor's race that he was unable to sleep at night. Finally, he said, he became "convinced that I was called of God to make that race." It would not be the last time Florida voters heard that claim.

Catts possessed the brazenness necessary to make some outlandish charges to gain the anti-Catholic vote. Alleging Catholic convents were used to store arms that would be used in an oncoming conflict with the US government, Catts vowed he would search convents and destroy those arms if elected governor.

Plainly, religious intolerance played a prominent part in the philosophy of life espoused by this former preacher turned jerk.

Another situation that greatly influenced the June primary election in 1916 was a new law allowing each voter to record a second choice vote on the ballot. This law was passed in hopes that it would eliminate a runoff election between the two candidates with the highest number of votes. The law stated that the winner would be the one who had the highest total of first and second choice votes. The confusion caused by the law not only affected the voters but also made it difficult for the election inspectors to count the votes. The results took so long in coming that there had to be a recount, followed by court approval. (The new law was changed back after the election.)

Catts and Knott were the candidates with the highest number of votes, but the count was extremely close. When the Supreme Court declared Knott the winner, Catts refused to give up. He switched to the Prohibition Party, and although it took four months of tumult, he finally got his name certified by the president of the Prohibition Party for the November election.

The Catts campaign was like no other. The candidate was not dependent on railways to reach voters, as all candidates had been in the past. He was the first to use a Model T Ford to reach towns that had never been visited by candidates before. Not only that, he installed a loudspeaker on his Ford, an attention-getter that never failed as he cruised through the streets looking for people. He stopped and began talking anytime he saw a few citizens he could buttonhole. Crowds gradually turned out in large numbers to hear him rave about how the Democratic Party had stolen the election from him, how he was the real people's candidate. Sympathetic crowds continued to grow.

Although anti-Catholicism predominated in his speeches, he did focus on some other issues, promising to lower taxes, reform election procedures, and establish industrial schools in major cities for boys and girls, but he always reverted to his religious conspiracy rants. The Jacksonville *Florida Times-Union* quoted him as saying, "Catts is going to open those convents for inspection. Catts is going to make them pay taxes; Catts is going to make those priests turn their collars right and marry good American girls."

He claimed he had information that a group of Catholics planned to assassinate him, and because of that, he carried two loaded revolvers, which he laid out where they could easily be seen by his audience. In his appeal to country audiences, he frequently claimed, "The Florida crackers have only three friends: God Almighty, Sears Roebuck, and Sidney J. Catts!" which always got a laugh and probably a few more votes.

Never one to give up the spotlight easily, Catts had one more attention-grabber. As the campaign ended, he telegraphed the

Governor Sidney Catts's inaugural parade, Tallahassee, Florida
STATE ARCHIVES OF FLORIDA, FLORIDA MEMORY, HTTP://FLORIDAMEMORY.COM/ITEMS/SHOW/128365

United States attorney with a request for federal poll watchers to prevent any unfair actions. It was one last emphasis on the concerns of fairness in the Catts campaign.

Much to the surprise of many Democrats, Catts won the election, inspiring the *New York Times* to describe the campaign as "one of the most spectacular gubernatorial campaigns ever waged in the United States." Furthermore, the *Times* stated the race was won with the aid of a Bible, two revolvers, and no money.

Preparations for the governor's inauguration were rather spectacular too. Although the impoverished Catts family had no clothes suitable for the ceremony, the whole family was provided with donated funds to buy new outfits. Five thousand people filled the Tallahassee streets to watch the parade of Confederate soldiers on horseback and a caravan of decorated cars, including one with Catts riding in it and a big sign on the side, proclaiming, THIS IS THE FORD THAT GOT ME THERE.

Not unexpectedly, the new governor started his administration with a bang. He relieved veteran government workers of their jobs and bestowed those jobs on folks who had helped in his campaign, in the process raising the ire of his enemies. The word "patronage" was heard frequently almost everywhere. Newspapers, particularly the Jacksonville *Florida Times-Union,* strongly criticized the governor's appointment of a number of his relatives. Congressman Frank Clark, an aspiring candidate for the next gubernatorial election, was especially active in attempts to embarrass Catts with his charges. Nasty exchanges between the two finally petered out, but the bad feelings endured.

Catts's dismissal of government officials became a prominent political issue, especially in Escambia County when he threatened to terminate a judge with whom he disagreed. Cooler heads prevailed before he moved on to Duval County, where some Jacksonville politicians asked Catts for an investigation into city corruption. The result was that another official, J. W. Rast, the county tax collector, lost his job and the governor's son-in-law, K. R. Paderick, was appointed to fill in. Rast had been accused but not convicted of embezzling public funds. When the time came to run for the position, Paderick lost decisively to the man he had replaced. Catts refused to accept defeat, however, and filed ten suits against Rast, who was finally found guilty of embezzling state and county funds and was sentenced to ten years in prison.

Catts dismissed many more officials, sometimes for good reason, sometimes simply to make room for people he wanted to appoint in their places. But he should also receive credit for many excellent suggestions he made to improve state government during his term, even if they were blocked from being passed.

The dominating anti-Catholic concern of the election campaign lost strength after the election. Governor Catts made one try at restricting Catholics by introducing a convent inspection law. After making several attempts at passing such a law, the legislature finally settled on a weakened inspection law, but it was never enforced, and Catts did not press for it any further.

The governor did come through in another episode that unquestionably qualified him as a Class A jerk, specializing in racism, religious bigotry, and anti-German feelings inspired by the onset of World War I. Many of the monks in the St. Leo Abbey near Tampa were German immigrants or of German ancestry. On more than one occasion, Governor Catts publicly speculated that the monks planned to supply Florida's African Americans with arms to stage a revolt favoring Kaiser Wilhelm. He assured listeners that this would be followed by Pope Benedict XV taking over Florida in order to move the Vatican to the United States and shutting down all Protestant churches. Outlandish and downright silly as it was, especially since the Pope was Italian, not German, and he was a well-known pacifist, some Germans left Florida for a friendlier environment. When denials were issued from the abbey, Catts moderated his rant.

As busy as the governor was, he very early on began to consider a run for United States senator when his term as governor would end. In June 1919, he made it official; he was in the race. His competition would be Duncan Fletcher, a lawyer, former mayor of Jacksonville, former state senator, and United States senator; Cary Hardee, past speaker of the House of Representatives; Van Cicero Swearingen, state attorney general and a friend of Catts; and Lincoln B. Hulley, President of Stetson University and senator from Volusia County.

Catts ran his campaign much as he did his first, touring in his Model T Ford in the backcountry without a firm schedule, stopping three or four times a day where it appealed to him and speaking wherever a few people stopped to listen.

In most of his speeches, he emphasized that he was an everyday Florida "Cracker" and stood up for people like himself. He frequently inserted racist statements in his talks and spoke strongly against the League of Nations, which was supported by his chief rival, Duncan Fletcher.

Catts opposed a proposal by the United States Public Health Service to locate a leprosarium on the island of Cedar Key, a project lukewarmly defended by Fletcher. Many state officials were likewise opposed to the project, fearing oyster beds would be polluted and escapees might spread the disease. Catts instigated a petition against the project, warning that Florida's chief rival for tourists, California, would spread a nickname change for Florida—from the Sunshine State to the Leper State. He also accused Fletcher of attempting to make the state a "dumping ground for lepers."

There were almost no newspapers promoting Catts in this election, not even many of the ones that had favored him in the governor's election. It did not bode well for Catts, and in the end he carried just three counties, all in the rural Panhandle. When Fletcher won the election by a wide margin, Catts was not a gracious loser.

He returned to DeFuniak Springs, bitter and broke. He bought a small spread of land to farm and plant an orchard. Dabbling in real estate occasionally, he also sold some insurance before he moved his family back to Georgia for a brief stay while he unsuccessfully tried to sell patent medicines and made futile attempts at a few more businesses ventures. In April 1921, he received notice that he was being indicted for allegedly taking bribes to pardon prisoners while he was governor. While the legal processes were proceeding, things got worse for Catts. In May, Pensacola authorities indicted him on charges of peonage, which was defined as holding persons in servitude as payment of a debt.

The first very complicated trial, conducted at Starke, in north Florida, in November 1921, resulted in acquittal for Catts. In November 1922, he was tried on federal peonage charges and was again acquitted.

He made a reasonably good effort at securing the Democratic nomination for governor in 1924 and again in 1928, but neither effort was good enough. Still unable to leave politics behind, he worked hard in 1928 to defeat the Catholic Al Smith in the presidential election.

Catts was tried once more, this time for counterfeiting, but again, he was cleared.

Cary Hardee, his former rival, defended him.

Catts died in 1936, having had his greatest triumph and his greatest defeat in the Sunshine State.

CHAPTER 10

111 Years of Child Cruelty

It's hard to believe that a state where children build castles on the sandy beaches, delight in magical amusement parks, splash in the sparkling ocean waters, and fish in the rivers and lakes is the same place where the juvenile correction system allowed children to be assaulted by adult males, cruelly punished for minor offenses, and denied medical care when it was indicated, all with no outside interference, for 111 years. With such a history, obviously some jerks had to be involved in this ugly chapter of Florida's past, described as the worst case of institutional child abuse in America.

In 2011, the Civil Rights Division of the US Department of Justice released a lengthy report focusing on conditions at the Dozier School for Boys and the Jackson Juvenile Offender Center in northern Florida. The report stated that even though the named reform schools, which were combined into the North Florida Youth Development Center, had been closed as of June 30, 2011, Florida's worthless, malfunctioning system had fostered dangerous situations in the state's juvenile prisons all over the state. Rather than helping boys to reform their lives in institutions that never lacked for jerks to inflict permanent scars on bodies and minds of boys as young as eight years old, the schools were guaranteed to make the boys' lives even worse.

It was in June 1897 that Florida lawmakers voted to establish a reform school where young delinquents could be "restored to the community with purposes and character fitting a good citizen." With an offer of twelve hundred acres of land plus a substantial sum of cash, the city of Marianna won the right to build and operate a new reform school. It opened in 1900, but three years later, an authorized committee reported that children were "in leg irons, just as common criminals," which in the committee's judgment was not the meaning of a "state reform school" as defined by the law that created it.

The Reform School Board, however, explained that since there were never enough guards, it was necessary somehow to deter the inmates to prevent their escape or their attempts to overpower the guards. Until 1930, when the children worked outdoors, they wore "step chains," a kind of bracelet welded onto each ankle and connected by a chain long enough for walking, but not for running.

So it began, and from then on, a year seldom passed without a report of some sort of brutalizing practice being committed at the school. For the first five years the school was in operation, there were no classes of any kind. The children either performed work on the school's farm or they were hired out to work in the convict lease system, which was brutal for adult prisoners and savage for children. Children under twelve years old were leased to phosphate and turpentine businesses and were expected to perform the same backbreaking work required of adult prisoners and were beaten severely if they did not do it well.

The bad news continued in 1914, when eight boys were incinerated in a dormitory fire that erupted in a dilapidated stove after staff members had locked all the doors leading outside before going into town to seek some fun.

The following year, when a Jackson County grand jury studied the situation, they concluded that the school employees had no experience in raising boys and "the young men having direct supervision of the boys were immoral and not proper persons to lead wayward boys toward reformation." Still, nothing was done.

When the school suffered a flu epidemic in 1918, the mayor of Marianna sent a telegram to authorities in Tallahassee proclaiming the "Industrial school in critical shape." So many boys were ill and without proper care that nurses and doctors were needed desperately, resulting in another black mark on the institution, another outrage unsolved.

The entire statewide system gained the attention of the public and could not be ignored when people learned about the cruel and inhumane treatment a young man named Martin Tabert suffered when he was trapped in the convict lease system.

In 1921, twenty-two-year-old Tabert, who had been working on his parents' North Dakota farm, set out on a journey to see some of the world. He ran out of money in Florida and was caught hopping a freight train in Tallahassee. Faced with paying a twenty-five-dollar fine or three months' hard labor, Tabert wired his family who sent the money in care of the sheriff, but through some kind of mix-up, the funds never arrived. Tabert was sent with other convicts to work in the swamps for the Putman Lumber Company.

Two months later, the first of our named jerks, Walter Higgenbotham, flogged the young man, who was ill with fevers and unable to work, with a leather strap at least fifty times. When Tabert was unable to get up from the beating, Higgenbotham gave him fifty more lashes. Tabert died five days later in his bunk, and although it took more than a year before the public learned of it, newspapers then rushed out stories about the event and about the convict lease system. Higgenbotham was tried for murder but acquitted.

As a result of the publicity about the case, flogging of prisoners was outlawed in 1923. Unfortunately and astonishingly, flogging continued in the boys' reform schools, and the atrocious conditions in the schools remained unchanged.

How many people in the small city of Marianna knew about the inhumane treatment of children going on in their midst? In that city in Jackson County, which called itself "the city of Southern charm," how could they not know? With a population of just 6,200, the town was born of a plantation society, where a lynching that made all the newspapers in 1934 was summarized by a white minister as having been accepted by the citizens "as a righteous act."

A new superintendent of the school, Arthur G. Dozier, was appointed in 1946. In one memorable speech, Dozier, a former schoolteacher, described his school as resembling a college campus more than a reform school.

An obvious attempt to reinforce that portrayal was carried out every year during the Christmas season, when the boys would be forced to build extravagant outdoor displays of lights and decorations, which attracted folks celebrating with their families to drive there from miles around. It was a grand display for the people who drove past—without stopping.

The population of the school, later renamed for Dozier, grew more crowded every year, eventually peaking with a population of nine hundred. As the school grew, problems also grew both in severity and in number. Stories of runaways, beatings, and whispers of deaths spread through Marianna, where most of the school employees lived. There weren't a lot of jobs in the county, and the ones at the school were grabbed as soon as any were open. Almost every family in Marianna had a member or knew of someone who worked at the school. Not all were guilty of abuse, but even those who remained silent would have to share some of the blame.

In 1958, a respected psychologist, Eugene Byrd, spent some time inside the school prior to testifying before a US Senate judiciary subcommittee. He observed some of the beatings, all of which were also witnessed by the superintendent; when questioned as to his opinion about the beatings, Byrd said that in his opinion, they constituted acts of brutality.

Governor Claude Kirk honored the school with a visit in 1968, the same year corporal punishment was declared illegal in state institutions. He observed the dreadful condition of the place—backed up sanitary facilities, holes in the roofs, lack of heat in winter—and he publicly stated that it was a training ground for criminals.

When rumors of cruelty surfaced, Dozier angrily denied that brutality existed in his institution, insisting it was simply a "clash in philosophy."

Dozier was not the only jerk involved. His strong right arm and school director, Robert W. Hatton, did not confine his work to a desk. He took frequent turns at cracking a whip on the backs of boys as young as ten. It was Hatton's whip that bloodied the back of a youngster who fifty years later would help to expose the cruel and savage nightmares in which boys lived or died for 111 years. There was another tormenter who would be vividly remembered through the years, never to be forgotten for two reasons. He was one of the most brutal of the school employees, and he had just one arm. However, one arm was all he needed to inflict the worst pain some of the victims would endure for the rest of their lives.

In all those years, how many lives were damaged or ruined by a few jerks? But clearly, *jerks* is too kind a word to describe the sadists who beat children until pieces of their flesh and their blood spattered the walls, their backsides were bruised black all the way to their knees, and parts of their underwear had to be picked from their torn flesh. Probably no one will ever know how many boys did not leave the place alive, but of those who did, how many were never able to live normal lives again? How many lives did they ruin—wives, children, parents—because many of them grew into men who could not control their rages or their sadness or their drinking, or their nightmares?

It was not until 2006 that Robert Straley, a businessman from Clearwater, Florida, contacted Michael O'McCarthy, a South Carolina journalist. As the two shared painful memories of the horrors they had both experienced at the Florida School for Boys, they agreed it was time for action. They wanted to bring together as many of the survivors of the school as they could and do whatever they could to see that no more boys would ever be admitted to their tragic group.

They got a great deal of help from Gus Barreiro, a former state legislator from Miami who had already earned a reputation as a champion of troubled boys and who, after leaving the legislature, assumed a position with the Department of Juvenile Justice. His first assignment for DJJ was to spend some time at the Arthur G. Dozier School for Boys to investigate the reports of cruelty and violence that were spreading far and wide.

He began his investigation by speaking at length with a number of Marianna citizens and was deeply disturbed to learn how those people seemed to be aware of the ugliness going on inside the school and yet nobody was doing anything about it. The forty-five days he spent at the school did nothing to brighten the picture, and still, the townspeople he spoke with admitted "hearing rumors," yet not one ever made an attempt to stop it. Anyone who ever lived in a small town knows such a secret would be impossible to keep.

Then, near the end of Barreiro's time at the school, someone mentioned a cemetery, something he had never heard anything about until then. The employee willingly took him the short distance behind the school to show him an easily overlooked clearing. Astonished, Barreiro counted thirty-one rusted pieces of pipes that were clumsily fashioned into unmarked crosses. He used his cell phone to photograph the site before returning to the school, where he tried to find out who was buried there. No one, it seemed, knew the answer. Yet the school tended the cemetery. Why?

The unanswered questions never ended, it seemed.

Barreiro was instrumental in enlisting Carol Marbin Miller, a journalist with an impeccable reputation, to write a front-page story for the *Miami Herald,* which led to an explosion of more stories in newspapers all over the country. The tragic stories of the White House Boys, as they wanted to be known, now men in their sixties and seventies, succeeded in getting everyone's attention.

They had a good reason to call themselves the White House Boys. The name is appropriate because these men were just boys when they were brutalized in a small, whitewashed, cinder-block building on the school grounds. They were beaten so badly that some lost consciousness, and when the beatings ended, some had to be taken to the infirmary for treatment. None of the men would ever forget that White House.

One of these men, Robert Straley, had spent his troubled childhood in a home where his truck-driving father was away most of the time because he preferred being on the road to being home with his wife, a woman given to extremely erratic behavior and wild rages. Robert began running away from home at an early age but was always brought back by the police. However, when he was about thirteen years old, he tried to escape but was caught, and when the police brought him home, his mother refused to take him back. That was how he ended up in the Florida School for Boys.

Michael O'McCarthy was fifteen when he was finally made to answer for the series of lesser infractions he'd committed, including cutting classes and petty theft. Ordered to spend a year at the school, he dreaded it. To a fifteen-year-old, a year seemed like an eternity, so he and a friend named Woody ran away as soon as they could, but they were caught and brought back. The school director, Robert Hatton, dragged them to the small, white concrete building behind the school, the White House. The boys all knew what went on there, even those who were among the fortunate few who had never been inside.

Michael was first. Woody waited outside.

The horror was always the same. The boy to be punished was made to lie on a filthy thin mattress that was stained with the blood and vomit and pieces of lips and tongues bitten off in agony by boys who went before. The boy was told to lie on his belly and grip the metal frame at the top of the bunk, and the beating would start. The whip tore into his flesh again and again and his blood spattered the walls, and he lost count of the number of lashes, but when Hatton finished and told him to get up, Michael couldn't move. Hatton said if he didn't move, he would start the beating all over again. So, somehow Michael moved and crawled to the hallway outside, where he leaned against the wall, listening to Woody's cries and screams, feeling Woody's blows almost as if they were his own. Michael never saw Woody again, never knew what happened to him. Did one of the rusty crosses mark his grave? Michael carried feelings of guilt the rest of his life because he thought he should have helped Woody, even though he knew he couldn't.

Bill "Willy" Haynes admits to being a rebellious young man when he was first sent to the Florida School for Boys in 1958. He also admits to still being afraid of the dark after some fifty years of memories of those beatings in the White House that smelled so bad it gagged him even before the beatings started. He can still

The infamous White House
ROGER DEAN KISER, SR.

see the paddle they used—two strips of quarter-inch leather, two inches wide and two feet long, with a strip of metal in between, attached to a round handle. The leather strips were perforated along the sides, and those little perforations filled with flesh and blood as the beatings progressed. Willy could never forget that some of the boys who went to the White House never came back.

"So what happened to them?" he asks. "Where are their bones buried? How many of them had no family at home to question the authorities?" He also says, "I feel in my heart that God must have a special seat in hell for people like the one-armed man, R. W. Hatton, Arthur Dozier, and others like them."

Richard Colon, an electrical engineer living in Baltimore, admits to having been a difficult teenager who survived eleven beatings in the White House. He wishes he could forget a day in the late 1950s when he was assigned a job in the school laundry room. He had just returned from a bathroom break to find one big clothes dryer running, tumbling and thudding and banging, with a black youth shut inside it, enduring the searing torture as his punishment for some infraction. Fearing what might happen to him if he tried to help the boy, Colon turned and walked away. He never heard what happened to the boy, but that boy was another who was not seen again after that day. Colon has been tormented ever since with the memory and the guilt for not helping, even though, realistically, he knows he could not have saved the other boy. He always wonders if that boy's final resting place was one marked with a corroded metal cross.

Roger Kiser was abandoned by his mother when he was four, sent to an orphanage where he never had enough to eat, and suffered the nightmare of being molested before he was transferred to the Arthur Dozier School for Boys in 1958. Once there, he said the beatings in the notorious White House were ungodly. He was so sure he would be killed with the thick, weighted-leather whip that he begged to be returned to the orphanage. As an adult, Kiser now spends all of his time working for juvenile justice and writing books about the horrors he and thousands of others suffered.

With so much publicity in the media, Florida authorities finally had no choice but to confront the outrage, despite the great extent of political maneuvering and evasion that went on.

Consequently, on October 21, 2008, a group of men mostly in their sixties gathered in front of an unimpressive, small, white-washed building with about fifty other people. There were people from the Department of Juvenile Justice, employees in uniform, reporters, and photographers. The men who called themselves the White House Boys were given permission to speak to the gathering for as long they wished.

They took turns telling of their torture and terror, each reliving it as he spoke, sometimes breaking down and having to be comforted for a few moments by other White House Boys before he could go on. There were few dry eyes anywhere.

Then Barreiro, who had completed the arrangements, told the gathering that a crepe myrtle tree would be planted at the side of the White House and a plaque would be installed to remember the hundreds, perhaps thousands, of boys who endured the tortures under the auspices of the State of Florida. It would read:

THE WHITE HOUSE PLAQUE
In memory of the children who passed through these doors, we acknowledge their tribulations and offer our hope that they have found some measure of peace.

May this building stand as a reminder of the need to remain vigilant in protecting our children as we help them to seek a brighter future.

Moreover, we offer the reassurance that we are dedicated to serving and protecting the youth who enter this campus, and helping them to transform their lives.

The White House
Officially Sealed
By the Department of Juvenile Justice
October 21, 2008

Higginbotham, Hatton, and Dozier have died. The one-armed man, now in his eighties, survives in Marianna, shielded by family and neighbors who have generously provided him with a fund if needed for a defense.

Michael O'McCarthy died from a heart attack in 2010, but the group of White House Boys he was instrumental in organizing has grown to more than five hundred men. Their sad work continues.

CHAPTER 11

Ben Hecht Buries a Treasure

Ben Hecht began his career at the *Chicago Daily Journal,* where he quickly became known as one of the best newspaper reporters in the country. He went on to write prize-winning short stories, essays, plays, books, his autobiography, and even poetry and a children's book. He would win the first Academy Award ever awarded for screenwriting. He wrote so many books, it's nearly impossible to make a count of them, but a rough estimate is thirty-five. Then, too, he either wrote or was involved in the writing of at least sixty-five scripts for major films, many of which became classics.

So, why would someone with such an amazing reputation take a chance on ruining it by orchestrating and pulling off a land swindle in Florida? In truth, Hecht was a talented man who had trouble living within his means—even though his means would have been considered more than generous by most people.

Hecht, born in New York City in 1894, was the son of Russian Jewish immigrants. His father was a garment cutter who moved the family to Racine, Wisconsin, where he started making ladies' dresses and then opened a store to sell them. Hecht's mother managed the store, while her husband spent a great deal of time traveling for the business. As a result, Hecht and his brother, Peter, were on their own more than most children. Hecht didn't mind though, because it allowed him to pursue many interests: first, a preoccupation with photography, then building and sailing a boat, and then learning to perform on a trapeze. Peter joined him in that venture, and both boys got to be so good at it that they performed with a circus one summer.

After Hecht graduated from high school, he moved to Chicago, where he stayed with relatives for a time while he tried something new—working as a reporter for the *Chicago Journal.* Never bashful, Hecht not only stretched the truth to come up with some

Ben Hecht

of the sensational stories he wrote, he went so far as to totally invent some facts and occasionally even whole tales, enabling him to get credit for reporting scoops. They were scoops because no one else had the nerve to invent them, but Hecht got away with it because his genuine writing talent resulted in stories readers enjoyed, even when knowledgeable sources produced evidence that disproved the stories. It most certainly was the behavior of a jerk, but somehow he escaped criticism.

In 1914, when Hecht decided he needed to make some major changes in his life, he moved over to the *Daily News,* where he hoped to get some fresh ideas and also a boost in his salary. His stable of acquaintances in the literary world increased, too, including people like Sherwood Anderson, Carl Sandburg, Theodore Dreiser, Vachel Lindsay, and the most important literary editor in Chicago and highly respected publisher of *The Literary Review,* Margaret Anderson. It was an exciting time, and Hecht loved being in the middle of what came to be called the Chicago Renaissance.

Also working at the *Daily News* was a young woman named Marie Armstrong, Chicago's only female reporter at that time. After a tumultuous, on-again, off-again romance, Hecht and Marie married on November 28, 1915. Neither of them was very good at balancing a budget, and both liked to entertain. As a result, they went deeper and deeper into debt in a hurry.

Hecht started to sell some of his short stories to *Smart Set,* one of the country's leading fiction magazines, published by H. L. Mencken. It was a feather in his hat, but unfortunately it paid very little and didn't help much with the couple's debts. His jerklike behavior made an appearance again when he brazenly sold a poem to a poetry magazine—a poem that was an obvious plagiarism of his acquaintance Carl Sandburg's poem "Fog." But again, Hecht got away with it.

More than anything else, Ben Hecht wanted to make a lot of money, and he didn't care who knew that about him. Accordingly, he wrote as much as he could, as fast as he could, and some of it was surprisingly good. Mostly his work was not considered excellent writing, but it sold to popular magazines. Writing a good novel takes most writers years. Hecht wrote one, *Eric Dorn,* in six months.

With the money he made from *Eric Dorn,* he paid off his debts and decided to leave journalism behind in order to concentrate on book and play writing. But then, when his former editor at the *News* asked him to come back to write a daily column about whatever he wanted to write about, Hecht couldn't refuse that flattering offer. It was the beginning of almost four years of his column, "1001 Afternoons in Chicago," which became the city's favorite news column, some of which he would later publish as a book.

He also took up with Rose Caylor, a writer employed at the *Chicago Daily News.* Actually, there were tales told about Hecht and several other women, but none seemed to last long. Rose was different. Before long, Hecht had a wife and a mistress, and the jerk in him considered it a suitable arrangement.

The "1001 Afternoons in Chicago" column ended when Hecht was fired due to bad publicity resulting from a threatened lawsuit involving Hecht and Pascal Covici, a publisher new to the business who had asked him for a flashy book—the spicier the better. Problems began when Hecht told Covici to send some copies to reviewers, and the post office received complaints about obscene materials being sent through the mail. The case was finally settled with fines for each of them, but Hecht, as usual, was never one to concede wrongdoing if he could avoid it; in this instance, he simply behaved as though it never happened.

That episode was not all that made it seem a good time for a drastic change in his life. The Chicago Renaissance was running out of steam, and Hecht was running out of money—again. New York beckoned.

Hecht and Rose made the move to New York City, where they settled into a Westside apartment. They occasionally joined other writers hanging out at the famous Algonquin, although Hecht considered the New York literati smug, silly, and inferior to the old gang from Chicago. He immersed himself in completing a stage play that was an immediate hit, and then began selling fiction to the *Saturday Evening Post, Redbook,* and *McClure's.*

In 1925, a writer friend, J. P. "Mac" McEvoy, made Hecht an interesting offer. Mac had been asked to rewrite a script for a movie that was to be filmed in Florida. The executives behind the movie weren't satisfied with the script as it was written. Attempts at revision had already been tried unsuccessfully by two other writers, and Mac hesitated to try the assignment on his own. He would feel more confident, he said, if Hecht would agree to join him in the project. His offer to pay the travel fees to Florida for Hecht and Rose sealed the deal.

For Hecht, the timing felt perfect. An out-of-control land boom had taken off in Florida at the start of the 1920s, assisted in part by the love affair Americans had developed with their newly acquired automobiles. It was no longer necessary to spend money for a train ride from the North down to Florida. Traveling in the family car with stops along the highway for campouts was doable for the middle class.

More people came for vacation, more people were enchanted with the land of sunny beaches and tropical climate, and more people wanted a piece of it. Real estate prices soared throughout much of the state, but particularly in the Miami area. Prospective buyers needed to act fast. Stories were told of properties being bought one day and sold the next for double or even triple the original price. A young newsboy was said to have swung a deal that netted him over one hundred-thousand dollars. The prevailing party atmosphere intoxicated everyone who came.

Hecht and Rose were a high-living couple who entertained a lot and were constantly broke. In addition, Hecht's frequent extramarital liaisons at expensive resorts and hotels added to his financial problems. He had already decided that making a lot of money was more important to him than sweating and straining to be a number-one novelist, and he wanted a piece of the Florida real estate pie.

In his autobiography, Hecht stated that when he, Rose, and Mac sailed into Miami, they couldn't help but feel flattered to be interviewed by newspaper reporters who apparently were assigned to approach anyone coming into the state who might be of interest. He used the interview as an opportunity to enthuse about Miami in case anyone he needed to impress should read the article in the newspaper.

Launches were used to move passengers from incoming large ships to shore because the harbor was not yet sufficiently developed to accommodate large ships. Hecht struck up a conversation with a fellow passenger on the ship while they waited to be taken ashore in a launch. As the two men talked, Hecht was able to glean some information about the land boom, specifically the names of the VIPs who were running the show. He made a written list of the names.

Later that evening at the Fleetwood Hotel where they were staying, Hecht met Walter O'Keefe, the young man who had the room across the hall from him. O'Keefe was the singer at a local nightclub and was a man-about-town who knew everyone.

During some talk with his new friend, Hecht learned which were the most important names on his list of movers and shakers and even finagled an introduction to the name at the top—Charles Ort, the president of the Key Largo Corporation, an organization consisting of a ninety-million-dollar group of pioneers. O'Keefe claimed to know that Ort had come to Miami with a few hundred dollars in his pockets, and within a couple of months he had fattened it up to about thirty million dollars.

Days later, O'Keefe arranged a meeting for Hecht at Ort's office in the Flagler building. When he entered Ort's office, Hecht noticed the newspaper with his flattering newspaper interview, one describing him as a "prince of litterateurs," spread out on Ort's desk. It was an excellent introduction, and Ort turned out to be an excellent contact.

When Hecht asked about Key Largo, Ort proceeded to expound on "the future playground of America—and Europe," emphasizing that the island was just forty miles south of Miami and envisioning future grand hotels, yachts, and casinos. There should be no difficulty in selling lots on Key Largo, Ort insisted. In fact, when word got out, there would most likely be another boom, a Key Largo boom this time.

Hecht agreed, adding that he had some ideas he thought could help sell those lots. Pleased, Ort invited him to the board of directors' meeting the next day, and Hecht promised to be there.

Back at the hotel, Hecht explained his scheme to McEvoy, adding that he planned to ask the Key Largo Corporation for $2,500 a week for a ten-week minimum. Mac thought it sounded great—so great, in fact, that he asked to be let in on whatever came over the $2,500. It was a deal, Hecht said.

Next morning, while Mac sat at his side, Hecht explained his scheme to the twelve heavy-hitters who all appeared eager to hear his ideas for expanding their wealth.

He began by reminding the directors that until the nineteenth century, a favored haunt of pirates, the Spanish Main, had included Florida and the shoreline all around the Gulf of Mexico, Central America, the northern coast of South America, as well as the Florida Keys. He emphasized that Key Largo was one of the most beautiful of the keys, and must surely have attracted pirates in need of places to hide their stolen treasures. It made sense, he said, that there must be millions of dollars of treasures still there.

Hecht's audience was enthralled.

His plan, he told them, was to arrange a treasure hunt, which would begin in New York City. It so happened that the ex-Kaiser's yacht was tied up at a dock on Long Island. He would have it chartered for fifty or so prominent female socialites, famous actors, or other celebrities and engage Paul Whiteman's orchestra to entertain them while they were sailed to Key Largo. He would have an old pirate treasure map for them to use for help in digging up some fabulous buried treasure. The treasure would have been buried previously, of course, so the women could be guided to it. Since prominent people would be involved, the resulting publicity would be stupendous, Hecht promised, and the result would be thousands of other treasure seekers descending on the island, their hearts set on buying lots.

It was easy to read the satisfaction on the faces of the millionaire board of directors. They wanted to know how much the initial outlay of funds would be, but before Hecht could answer, Mac said that being that he was the business side of the partnership, he could tell them that it would take five thousand dollars a week for twelve weeks.

The board of directors smiled and gave their approval.

Mac quickly added that there would be the added expenses for the hunt—the gems and gold and silver pieces, hiring someone to bury them, rental fee for the yacht, plus costs of food, entertainment, and for an office and office supplies in Miami for Hecht and himself.

The board nodded again. A contract was signed, no problem.

Hecht and Mac set up a huge office in the Fleetwood Hotel where they had been staying. Since they had to pay their office staff from their own pay, they hired only two people, a secretary and Charles Samuels, the newspaper reporter who had interviewed them when they arrived in Miami. Samuels would be a loyal news reporter for them.

While Mac set off for New York to see about renting the ex-Kaiser's yacht and engaging ladies for the treasure hunt, Hecht and Rose enjoyed the amenities of the Fleetwood Hotel, Ort's two boats, which he placed at their disposal, and the nearby beach. Hecht also wrote a kind of advertising newspaper, the *Key Largo Breeze,* which Ort read to his sales staff, hoping to inspire them.

However, while Hecht was enjoying himself in the sunshine, things were not going well in New York, where Mac reported that he wasn't able to line up any socialites or celebrities for the treasure hunt. Not only that, Samuels found out the Key Largo Corporation Board of Directors was getting impatient for some action. It was time for Mac to return and assist in starting Plan B.

They needed to round up some Spanish doubloons, which they did. They tried without success to find an old treasure chest, so they shopped around and found two eighteenth-century Spanish vases that were about five feet tall and weighed a hundred pounds.

Samuels, assigned to find someone to fill the role of the discoverer of the pirate treasure, returned with Cap'n Loftus, a native beachcomber who, for a hundred dollars, agreed to pass himself off as the finder of the Spanish treasure. They felt sure he would not give them any trouble, as he could not read or write and was unable to name the current president of the United States.

Hecht hired a boat to haul Samuels, Rose, and himself to Key Largo with the vases and doubloons. Once ashore, they broke the vases and planted their treasure and, knowing photographers would descend on the area when the story got out, scattered a few old coins nearby for effect.

Back in Miami, Hecht sent telegrams to two hundred editors, asking if they wanted the story of a half-million-dollar treasure discovered in Key Largo. When about half of them responded in the affirmative, he sent them the story, and in less than twenty-four hours, reporters began to arrive from nearby Southern states, followed shortly by swarms of people from everywhere, armed with tents and digging equipment.

Salesmen from the Key Largo Corporation rushed to the island, armed with sales contracts, and before a week had passed, they sold more than a million dollars' worth of lots in the bug- and snake-infested jungle. The elated Walter Ort and his associates offered Hecht another contract, but he was beginning to be bored and was ready to exit the Sunshine State. Then, too, he suspected the boom was about over. He openly confided this to Ort and his associates when he refused their offer.

Actually, Hecht had been suspecting the end was in sight for some time and had not been banking his money. He carried it all on his person, which was why everyone who saw him thought he was putting on weight. Increasingly, crowds could be seen swarming over area real estate offices, screaming and demanding their money back.

Hecht sent ten thousand dollars to Marie to pay for a divorce, quit his job with the Key West Corporation, married Rose, and headed back to New York. The next time he heard anything about

Ort, he learned Ort and his wife were sleeping in their car in a parking lot.

Hecht moved on, finally realizing his desire to make big money when he accepted an offer to write scripts for films. Once established in Hollywood, the financial benefits were immediate. And they kept on coming. His first script for *Underworld* was a smash hit that paid him ten thousand dollars right off the bat—and that was just the beginning.

In May 1929, he received the first Oscar ever awarded for a screenplay and followed up with scripts for many of the important movies being made, including *Gone with the Wind, Mutiny on the Bounty,* and *Wuthering Heights.*

Like many other jerks in Florida history, Hecht wasn't all bad. Until the rise of Nazism, he had almost nothing to do with either Judaism or politics. In the 1940s, that changed when he met Peter Bergson, a Zionist who came to the United States to raise funds and publicize the need to rescue European Jews. Hecht involved himself wholeheartedly in fund-raising and making speeches to raise awareness of the plight of Jewish refugees and the necessity for the establishment of the State of Israel.

He wrote the screenplay for *A Flag is Born,* which opened in New York City, starring Marlon Brando and Paul Muni, and was attended by Eleanor Roosevelt and New York City Mayor William O'Dwyer. The play, sponsored by a group of militant Jewish activists known as the Bergson Group, was not a critical hit, but it was a financial hit—enough to enable the group to buy a captured German ship, which was renamed the SS *Ben Hecht* and eventually became the flagship of the Israeli Navy.

Perhaps Hecht's previous frequent jerk-like behavior, some of it in Florida, can be at least partially atoned for by his late-life anti-Nazi efforts. He died of a heart attack on April 18, 1964. The future prime minister of Israel, Menachem Begin, offered Hecht's eulogy at the Temple Rodeph Sholom in New York City.

CHAPTER 12

Pepper, Ball, and Gorgeous George

Elections seem to bring out the worst in some people. When political campaigns commence, jerks come out of the woodwork, and otherwise reasonable people frequently exhibit behavior that would make them feel ashamed any other time. The Florida election of 1950 has been described as the most bitter, ugliest, and dirtiest campaign in Florida history. The respected television commentator David Brinkley offered that in his opinion it was the dirtiest contest of all time in the entire nation's history, an impressive statement, especially considering the knowledgeable source. Accordingly, an amazing number of otherwise decent citizens acted like jerks during that campaign.

Two of the major players in the election drama were Ed Ball, a businessman who never held a public office and who preferred to operate behind the scenes, and Senator Claude Pepper, who was way out in front. Waiting in the wings to run against Pepper was the senator's former protégé, George Smathers.

Edward Ball was born in Virginia in 1888 and showed an intense interest in making money at a very young age. He had no desire to hold elected office himself. Instead, his power in Florida politics resulted from his growing influence in business concerns, essentially as a representative for Alfred I. duPont's business affairs. Ball's sister, Jessie, was duPont's third wife, and in 1926, she and her husband left Delaware, the home state of his enormously wealthy and powerful family, to establish their residence in Jacksonville, Florida, far from Delaware tax collectors. With the assistance of his brother-in-law, duPont rapidly acquired thirteen thousand acres of land in the Panhandle and then built a paper mill there at Port St. Joe. Together, Ball and duPont formed Almours Securities, Inc., the corporate tent for the Florida duPont resources. They concentrated chiefly on real estate and banking, gradually acquiring more than a million acres of land and a prime interest in the Florida National Bank. As they acquired other banks, they joined them all together to form the Florida National Group, which became the second-strongest bank in the state, second only to Barnett Bank.

When the stock market crashed in 1929, Henry Flagler's famed Florida East Coast Railway (FEC) fell on increasingly hard times. Ball, working in Washington, DC, for the duPont-Ball interests, made up his mind. He would get control of the FEC. However, he encountered formidable opposition from Senator Claude Pepper, who made up his mind to keep that from happening.

Pepper and Ball at first maintained a politely cordial relationship, differing on issues, but without the overt hostility that would become evident in their later relations.

Approximately eighteen years after Flagler's death, Ball purchased the Florida East Coast Railway for the duPont Trust. As executor of the estate and at the urging of his sister, Ball took control of the duPont Trust and all other business interests in the approximately thirty four million dollars estate after Alfred duPont's death in 1935. Ball was most likely Florida's largest landowner, the owner of the most banks and the most railroads—and, it would follow, the leading political power in the state. As such, it is certain he did not look kindly on Franklin Delano Roosevelt and his New Deal.

In sharp contrast, Claude Pepper was born in 1900 into a family of poverty-stricken Alabama sharecroppers. As a young boy, he picked cotton, plowed fields, and then worked in a steel mill before he acquired a bank loan to attend the University of Alabama. While a student at college, he worked a 4:00 a.m. to 7:00 a.m. shift in the university boiler room and also served a noncombat stint in the Student Army Training Corps in World War I. His connection to military service enabled him to attend Harvard Law School, where he sharpened his already impressive speaking skills and graduated in the top third of his class.

He opened his first law practice when he moved to Perry, Florida. It was the fulfillment of a childhood dream when he was elected to the Florida House of Representatives in 1929, but that dream ended abruptly when he lost his bid for reelection.

Undaunted, he moved to Tallahassee, where he opened a new law office in the state's capital. Still interested in politics, Pepper determined to try again, but he lost again in the primary election for the United States Senate in 1934. Just two years later, the determined young man won a special election following the death of Senator Duncan Fletcher.

Red-headed and usually described as homely, Pepper was nevertheless an exciting public speaker and an avid New Dealer, who enthusiastically allied himself with Franklin Delano Roosevelt, and with unions, the elderly, and liberals. He was outspoken in promoting an alliance with the Soviet Union, certain that the United States would not be able to avoid involvement in the war that was going on in Europe against Hitler.

He won reelection in 1938, and in making his first trip to Europe with his wife, Mildred, he was able to observe Hitler up close, although he did not meet him personally. Convinced that war would be unavoidable for the United States, Pepper strongly supported lend-lease legislation to send war planes to Great Britain.

His close, mutually supportive relationship with President Roosevelt did not carry over when Harry Truman moved into the White House. In fact, Pepper had first supported Henry Wallace for president, and when that did not work out, he supported Dwight D. Eisenhower as a Democratic candidate before Eisenhower decided not to run. Although Pepper finally did do some campaigning for the party ticket, his support for Truman was decidedly lukewarm, and obviously Truman must have been aware of it.

World War II was winding down in 1945, and owing to his position on the Senate Foreign Relations Committee, Pepper traveled with several other committee members first to Europe, then on to Moscow, where the group conferred with Joseph Stalin. Pepper, who believed that calm, civil treatment of the Soviets would encourage similar action on their part, did not envision the emerging threat from Communism as the other committee members did, and as did President Truman.

Although new to his office, Truman demonstrated he would take a harder stance toward Soviet imperialism than Roosevelt had. Even so, Pepper felt satisfied with his one-hour meeting with Stalin, not knowing it would come back to haunt him for a long time to come.

The other major player in the drama of the 1950 election was handsome, young George A. Smathers, who was born in Atlantic City, New Jersey, in 1913. His father was a practicing attorney, and many of his family members were involved in politics. When George was six years old, the Smathers family moved to Miami, where George excelled scholastically and in sports, both in grade school and in high school. He then attended the University of Florida, where he captained teams in basketball, track, and debating and won other awards and honors. He had grown into a personable, handsome, popular young man. While he was president of the student body, he contacted Claude Pepper, prevailing on him to make Smathers his campaign manager on the university campus for the older man's run for the Senate.

Smathers graduated with a degree in law and then served with the United States Marines in the South Pacific in World War II. As hostilities there wound down, he was assigned to legal duties in the service. He sought and received an early discharge—with the help of Senator Pepper.

In 1946, soon after Smathers returned home to Florida, he was elected to the US House of Representatives, where he served two terms. Outgoing and charming during his time in the House, he made many friends among politicians who would become famous, among them John F. Kennedy, Richard Nixon, and Lyndon Johnson.

After easily being reelected to the Florida House in 1948, Smathers showed no qualms two years later about running against his old mentor, Claude Pepper, for the US Senate seat.

He definitely made up his mind about it after he received a call to meet with President Truman in the White House.

Their relations were cordial, Truman having spent leisure time at Key West in Smathers's home district, but young congressmen did not ordinarily receive invitations to the White House so early in their careers. Smathers later related that after some preliminary small talk, the president bluntly told him, "George, I want you to beat that [expletive] Claude Pepper."

So began the memorable 1950 campaign, one inspiring much jerk-like behavior.

Beloved by many of his constituents, Pepper also had much going against him. Whites in the South were driven to preserve segregation, and it was a well-known fact that when Pepper served his term in the Florida House, there had been a great to-do concerning President Herbert Hoover's wife. She had once invited Jessie DePriest, a black congressman's wife, to a White House tea. Claude Pepper voted against a resolution on the floor condemning Mrs. Hoover. Also unusual for a Southern representative, he pushed for anti–poll tax legislation and helped to mobilize an alliance of organized labor and blacks, which inspired hostility among businessmen, Edward Ball among them.

As a liberal United States senator, Pepper supported FDR without any reservations. He alienated nearly the entire medical profession by pushing for universal health care way back then, and he was involved in helping to launch the now-standard forty-hour workweek.

But then, too, while the rest of the country was gradually losing its enthusiasm for support of the Soviets, Pepper continued to uphold a more amicable position toward them, praising Stalin and even appearing at peace rallies with American Communists.

Tensions between the NATO allies and the Soviet Union began to escalate soon after World War II ended, resulting in the start of the Cold War, with accompanying Cold War politics. A case in point was that Richard Nixon won his California Senate seat after a campaign during which he described his female opponent as "pink down to her underwear."

The junior Wisconsin senator, Joseph McCarthy, started his path to fame in 1950, when he accused the State Department of employing two hundred communists in its midst and claimed to have their names. McCarthy did not specifically accuse Pepper, but with the changing attitude toward the Soviets, Pepper's longstanding promotion of that nation did not sit well with many people. Few people were sympathetic with his past record of Soviet appeasement. His previous meeting with Joseph Stalin was mentioned frequently, as were his admiring descriptions of the Soviet leader.

Pepper's rival sprang into action—with Ed Ball's money behind him. Smathers did not lack for ammunition.

He opened with a speech that left no doubt as to how he planned to conduct his campaign. Some of the more memorable quotes stand out:

> *The leader of the radicals and extremists is now on trial in Florida. Arrayed against him will be loyal Americans who believe in free enterprise, who want to preserve their right to think, to work and to worship as they please. Standing against us will be certain Northern labor bosses, all the Communists, all the Socialists, all the radicals and the fellow travelers. . . . Surely we will not turn from the noble principles of Jefferson and Jackson to the careermen of Communism. . . . Florida will not allow herself to become entangled in the spiraling web of the Red network. The people of our state will no longer tolerate advocates of treason. . . . The outcome can truly determine whether our homes will be destroyed; whether our children will be torn from their mothers, trained as conspirators and turned against their parents, their home and their church. . . . I stand for election on the principle of the Free State against the Jail State.*

Smathers turned against his older benefactor with a vengeance. Speeches like the one above planted suggestions of McCarthyism in the minds of many.

But while Smathers tied Pepper to Stalin, Pepper likewise seldom missed an opportunity to refer to the "duPont lawyer," a reminder of the force and influence of the duPont wealth in his competitor's campaign. Pepper also rarely missed the chance to evoke the mental picture of an ungrateful young man betraying the older man who had helped him out and that same young man selling out to the moneyed powers, the very famous duPont and Ball, of course, leading the pack.

In one speech, Pepper said of Smathers that "the duPont crowd got hold of him in 1949 and offered him a vast campaign fund to make his race against me and the people."

Neither side lacked for jerk-like behavior. In fact, there was so much of it that it inspired a legend that persists today. It was said Smathers had a special speech for when he spoke to poor uneducated Florida Crackers, hoping to stir their enthusiasm and knowing they could not understand big words. Part of the speech went like this:

> *Are you aware that Claude Pepper is known all over Washington as a shameless extrovert?*
>
> *Not only that, but this man is reliably reported to practice nepotism with his sister-in-law, and he has a sister who was once a thespian in wicked New York.*
>
> *Worst of all, it is an established fact that Mr. Pepper, before his marriage, habitually practiced celibacy.*

Claiming innocence, Smathers offered ten thousand dollars to anyone who could prove the speech was his, but no one stepped up. He denied having anything to do with it, but *Time* magazine printed the whole thing, referring to it as a "yarn." Their reporters were said to have concocted it, but they, too, denied it. Nevertheless, the legend followed Smathers to his grave.

In his autobiography, Pepper stated that Ed Ball and some other businessmen routinely referred to him as "Red Pepper," had raised millions of dollars for the campaign, and rounded up every photograph taken of him with black people to use against him. He also said they had paid blacks to wait for him after he made a speech. The blacks would congratulate him on his excellent speech and shake his hand while waiting hired photographers snapped a photo to be passed around among the white supremacists as evidence of where Pepper stood on civil rights. Whether or not the accusation was true, one picture of Pepper with Paul Robeson, the famous black singer and communist supporter, circulated widely in many newspapers.

The label "Red Pepper" began to appear more and more. Even the All-American, down-home *Saturday Evening Post,* with its huge following, printed a story about the politics of the "spell-binding pinko Senator Pepper," too late in the campaign for an effective response.

But probably the publication with the most negative effect was published shortly before election day. Called *The Red Record of Senator Claude Pepper,* the forty-nine-page booklet was also published too late for a response. It contained parts of Pepper's speeches, edited so that out-of-context portions of some of his remarks stood out. Photographs of him with Robeson and others with Henry Wallace, the far-left politician, were highlighted, along with half-truths. Since television was not yet a major factor in election campaigning, the booklet was distributed widely one week before the election in hopes of creating a negative reaction. In his autobiography, Pepper said he later learned the shipment of the booklets to Miami alone weighed nine tons.

Several sources attributed the booklet to Lloyd C. Leemis, a Jacksonville writer and former FBI agent. Pepper claimed that Ball, through Smathers, paid the salary of two former FBI agents to follow Pepper everywhere, under orders to report where he spoke, what he said, etc. Not surprisingly, Smathers denied having anything to do with it.

As previously mentioned, there was no scarcity of jerks involved in the 1950 election. And what was also not surprising, on May 2, 1950, when the great number of Florida voters went to the polls, was that Claude Pepper was soundly defeated.

Smathers, who became known as "Gorgeous George" to friends and enemies alike, went on to serve three terms in the Senate. During his years in the Senate, he pushed for strengthening relations with Latin American countries in an attempt to stop the spread of Communism, at the same time raising early warnings about Fidel Castro. Maintaining his Southern roots, he remained a segregationist, unfailingly voting against all civil rights legislation.

He was one of eighteen Southern senators to sign the Southern Manifesto, which condemned the Supreme Court decision

Smathers leads over Pepper in votes.
STATE ARCHIVES OF FLORIDA, FLORIDA MEMORY

to desegregate public schools. He voted against the Civil Rights Act and against Thurgood Marshall's promotion to the Supreme Court. He offered to pay the bail for Martin Luther King when he was incarcerated, but only if King would leave Florida.

At the end of his third term, Smathers returned to Miami, where he opened a law office and became a successful business-man. He donated twenty four million dollars to the University of Florida library system, now known as the George A. Smathers Libraries. He also practiced law periodically in Washington, DC, until his death in 2007.

Shortly after the election, while Pepper was still Florida's sen-ator, both he and Ed Ball attended a dinner meeting of the Florida Industrial Council. When with a touch of sarcasm Pepper congrat-ulated Ball on "his" victory, Ball responded that it was good to win "the last round." Pepper answered that it might not be the last round. At that, ending all attempts at civility, according to Pepper, Ball shouted, "Claude, if you ever run for public office in Florida again, we'll lick you so bad you'll think this time was a victory."

Ball returned to overseeing the interests of the duPont Trust, by then valued at two billion dollars. He lived to be ninety-three, surviving his sister by eighteen years. Her Jessie duPont Fund was worth seventy five million dollars and his own estate was between seventy five dollars and two hundred million dollars. Except for several small gifts, Ball, very un-jerk-like, left his entire estate to the Nemours Foundation, a pediatric health organization with hospitals in Delaware, New Jersey, Pennsylvania, and Florida.

Claude Pepper's return to private life was difficult. The cam-paign had taken a toll on his finances, so he thought it prudent to open a law office in Tallahassee and another in Miami. He had loved his time in government, and thoughts of returning to it were never far from his mind. He made another run for the Senate in 1958, but was disappointed to be defeated again.

Back in Miami, as his practice grew steadily for twelve years, so too did the population of Miami and Dade County. In fact, the population grew so much that the Third Congressional District was created, and Pepper easily became its representative. He gladly remained so for the remainder of his life, one of the very few ever to be elected to the House after a career in the Senate.

The "grand old man of Florida politics" made the cover of *Time* magazine twice and was presented with the Presidential Medal of Freedom by President H. W. Bush four days before he died in 1989 at the age of eighty-eight.

CHAPTER 13

The Trial of
Marjorie Kinnan Rawlings

Marjorie Kinnan told stories all her life. Among her many happy memories were summer evenings spent playing vigorous games with neighborhood children and then sitting on the church steps with everyone gathered around her, eagerly awaiting her stories. She knew they must have enjoyed them, because they always came back for more. Born in Washington, DC, in 1896, to a mother who was a schoolteacher and a father who was a lawyer and dairy farmer, Marjorie enjoyed an idyllic childhood.

She began making up tales as soon as she learned to how to write. Encouraged by winning a two-dollar prize for a children's story she sent to the *Washington Post,* she submitted more, won more prizes, and then was named assistant editor of her school magazine. Winning a seventy-five-dollar prize for a short story in *McCall's* magazine was a major triumph of her high school days, but the death of her beloved father when she was a senior in high school devastated her, as it did her mother and her younger brother, Arthur.

Because of his close friendship with Senator La Follette of Wisconsin, her father had planned to send both his children to the University of Wisconsin. Determined to honor his wishes, the three remaining members of the Kinnan family moved to Madison, Wisconsin, near the campus where Marjorie enrolled as an English major.

She earned good grades, made Phi Beta Kappa in her junior year, and won prizes for her writing and praise for her editorials, stories, poems, book reviews, and other articles for the Wisconsin *Literary Magazine,* where she worked with the young man who would later become her husband, Chuck Rawlings.

Marjorie Rawlings at Cross Creek

They both graduated in 1918, one year after the United States declared war on Germany. Chuck enlisted in the army and fulfilled his basic training before being stationed for the rest of his enlistment on Long Island. After his discharge, he returned to Rochester, his family's hometown.

Hoping to launch her writing career, Marjorie moved to New York City, but she found little success. Similarly, Chuck made no headway with his writing in Rochester. They married in 1919, and then, thanks to some friends pulling strings in Louisville, Kentucky, they were both hired by the *Courier-Journal,* Chuck as a reporter, Marjorie as a feature writer.

It turned out to be a disappointing move for them and their meager hopes for their future in journalism. After two frustrating years, they moved back to Rochester, where Chuck took a job in sales for his father's shoe factory, a job that made it necessary for him to be on the road much of the time. Marjorie tried unsuccessfully to sell short stories while she wrote feature articles for city newspapers.

In 1923, they both suffered great losses. Chuck's father died, and a few months later, Marjorie's mother passed on. With the careers of the newlyweds not going well, the added stress put tremendous strains on their marriage.

They thought it would be a good time for a vacation, and since Chuck's brothers, Jimmy and Wray, were working in Florida, Marjorie and Chuck signed up for a cruise down the coast to Jacksonville. They were met there by a curt but friendly woman, Zelma Cason, who took them to a hotel to rest while they waited for Chuck's brothers. Zelma lived with her family in Island Groves, where Jimmie and Wray operated a filling station and made a stab at selling real estate. The brothers took Marjorie and Chuck inland to show them the part of Florida few people bothered to visit, including little Island Grove.

Marjorie and Chuck were fascinated. The remoteness, the beauty of the rivers, the lakes, the majestic live oaks, and the smell of the orange groves worked a kind of magic. They were sure it would be the perfect place for them to write. While they returned north, Wray and Jimmie scouted the area and found a seventy-four-acre property with a farmhouse, a tenant house, a barn, assorted animals, thirty acres of orange groves, a grove of pecan trees, and a number of tangerine and grapefruit trees—all for nine thousand dollars. Marjorie was able to cover a generous down payment from her inheritance, and in 1928 the young couple moved to Cross Creek.

While the Rawlings brothers worked the groves and grounds and repaired the house, Marjorie cooked three meals a day, cared for the animals that came with the sale, washed the clothes in an old iron pot, and planted a garden, all without benefit of a water heater or indoor privy.

Despite the endless hard work, Marjorie and Chuck kept on writing. Marjorie delighted in her surroundings and in the people she met. The unfamiliar animals and birds and the exotic trees, shrubs, and flowers—she studied it all, making notes of the names and minute details about everything. She did the same with the people as she got to know them.

Zelma Cason, the census taker for Alachua County, invited Marjorie to accompany her on her rounds. As the two women got to know each other, Marjorie learned that Zelma lived with her family in Island Grove and managed her brother's orange grove, a tough job even for a strong woman. At the same time, she frequently worked in her census office during the week.

The women spent several days horseback riding through swamps, across the River Styx, past a turpentine still, and all around Orange Lake. Along the way, Zelma laughed and joked with the people she met, commiserated with them when they confided their illnesses, and offered to send them medicines. She introduced Marjorie to the families and confided their life histories to her afterward.

A year after arriving in Florida, Marjorie sent a book of vignettes about the fascinating people who were her neighbors to *Scribner's Magazine*. She called it "Cracker Chidlings" and was excited when she received $150 for it.

But at the time the book appeared in stores, Marjorie had to undergo an appendectomy. While she was in bed recuperating, the angry mother of a young man Marjorie had described in a rather negative way in the book came to her home to settle the score. Luckily, Zelma was there to calm things down and rescue the author. When Marjorie was ambulatory, Zelma accompanied her to the woman's house to apologize.

Marjorie's writing caught the attention of famed *Scribner's Magazine* editor Maxwell Perkins, who wanted to see more of her work and was clearly impressed with her talent for bringing to life the determination and heroic survival of characters who endured lifelong deprivation and pain. She wrote about the lush beauty of the land, but she wrote, too, about the torture of mosquitoes, termites, snakes, and ants.

Offering enthusiastic encouragement, Perkins suggested she write a novel, and using his helpful suggestions, she did. Not only was Marjorie's first novel, *South Moon Under,* chosen by the Book-of-the-Month Club, her short stories began to sell then too.

Although Chuck had started to sell some of his articles and stories, his achievements were unimpressive compared to hers. He did not take it well, and gradually his criticisms of Marjorie and her work gnawed at their marriage. Chuck left Cross Creek, and the union ended in 1933.

The breakup left Marjorie sad but relieved too, knowing the almost constant stream of criticism was over.

In spite of being solely responsible for running the farm, Marjorie found time to write, turning out short pieces for magazines and another novel, *Golden Apples,* in 1935, in between chores of milking cows and feeding chickens. Then, too, she and her brother, Arthur, had remained very close, and though he lived far away, she was always the good big sister, offering moral and financial support when his life didn't turn out so well.

She made time to get to know her neighbors, who charmed her, and gradually she started to entertain visiting authors and others she met through Maxwell Perkins. She also began work on another book, one suggested by Perkins. It would turn out to be the one she became most famous for, the one she called *The Yearling*.

Promptly chosen by the Book-of-the-Month Club, it was made into a movie and won a Pulitzer Prize. With accolades pouring in, *The Yearling* was declared a classic.

Marjorie enjoyed the excitement and savored the opportunities resulting from the publication of *The Yearling*. She gave lectures at the University of Florida and became acquainted with many fascinating people, including a hotel manager named Norton Baskin.

As a result of so much publicity, magazines clamored for her short stories, and Scribner put together an anthology of them, *When the Whippoorwill,* another publishing success. As for the author, her relationship with Norton Baskin deepened, and they married before she was on to her next major writing project.

Her relationship with the people she lived among likewise deepened. She was always available when neighbors or people who worked for her were in dire straits. When her grove overseer was shot, she paid his hospital bills. When her housekeeper's daughter got married, Marjorie paid for the wedding. She was always there when someone was sick or hungry, and she outdid herself at Christmas, having the time of her life passing out food, clothes, and toys.

It felt only natural when, with suggestions from Maxwell Perkins, she made her next project a collection of new stories about her Florida home and the neighbors she had grown to love. *Cross Creek,* published in 1942, was an immediate hit.

However, while she was writing the pieces about her neighbors, Marjorie contacted Perkins, saying she had used some real names in *Cross Creek* and needed his advice. "These people are my friends and neighbors, and I would not be unkind for anything, and though they are simple folk, there is the possible libel danger to think of," she said, asking for his opinion.

Perkins doubted there would be "any real danger" but said the final decision would be hers. He particularly liked the chapter on Zelma and suggested working with her more.

Thinking some personal visits might help to solve the problem, Marjorie did visit some neighbors to ask how they would feel about having their real names in her book. Although most said they were proud to be included, others were lukewarm but did not seriously object. Some agreed with her friend, Dessie Smith, who said, "The truth is the truth!"

Unbeknownst to Marjorie, another woman she considered a friend, Zelma Cason, did object, but not to her face. Zelma quietly canvassed the neighborhood, seeking allies. Apparently, a few other neighbors were a bit annoyed at being named in the book, but not so much that they wanted to do anything about it.

Possibly Marjorie felt secure in her friendship with Zelma, not only because of a boat and camping trip they had taken together but also because Zelma's brother, Dr. T. Z. Cason, was Marjorie's personal physician. Then, too, when Zelma made frequent trips out of town to attend to a position she held with the Florida State Welfare Board, Marjorie often visited Zelma's mother, who was in poor health and didn't get out much. Marjorie had no reason to doubt their friendship.

Thinking Zelma would be pleased with her part in the book, very soon after it was published Marjorie presented her with a copy, personally autographed to her "good friend." She was shocked when Zelma tossed it aside, saying Marjorie had humiliated her, made her look like a hussy.

Of course Marjorie knew about Zelma's temper. She was known throughout the neighborhood for being moody, profane, and sharp-tongued, and for being one who, when crossed, cussed a blue streak so loud she could be heard a quarter of a mile away. Still, her reaction was shocking and hurtful.

In tears, Marjorie tried to explain she meant no harm, that everyone she talked to who had read the chapter about Zelma thought it was a cute description. Zelma did not. She raged to more than one neighbor about the description in the very first paragraph. It was as follows:

Zelma is an ageless spinster resembling an angry and effi-
cient canary. She manages her orange grove and as much
of the village and county as needs management or will sub-
mit to it. I cannot decide whether she should have been a
man or a mother. She combines the more violent charac-
teristics of both and those who ask for or accept her mani-
fold ministrations think nothing of being cursed loudly at
the very instance of being tenderly fed, clothed, nursed or
guided through their troubles.

Two months later, the Pulitzer Prize winner was being sued in
Alachua County Circuit Court by her former friend, who claimed
libel and invasion of privacy.

Marjorie could not stop the seething confusion that nagged at
her. Over and over she wondered, "Why?" Why was Zelma doing
this? She thought they were friends. Was Zelma jealous of her success, the money, the fame, the opportunities for more, the celebrities now in her life . . . the money? Was it Zelma's intention to
get some of the money Marjorie was suddenly accumulating? She
didn't want to believe that, but could it possibly be true?

Although the court dismissed Zelma's claims, the Florida
Supreme Court would reverse the dismissal of the lower court concerning the invasion of privacy. The unpleasantness was not over.

To confuse things even further, Marjorie's attorney, Philip
May, heard that soon after *Cross Creek* was in bookstores, Zelma
had brandished a copy where she worked as a caseworker for the
State Welfare Board, all smiles and obviously pleased with her
sudden fame.

As if she didn't have enough chaos in her life, Marjorie was also
suffering from bouts of diverticulitis, which required occasional
brief hospitalizations. In addition, World War II was underway,
and the last straw for Marjorie was when Norton, who had wanted
to serve in the armed forces but was rejected, told her he had
signed up to be an ambulance driver and would be overseas, driving dangerously close to battle. A lifelong patriot, Marjorie had

been trying to do her part for the war effort, but her concern for Norton almost paralyzed her.

Through it all, she did somehow keep on writing, even producing another book that quickly became a favorite, *Cross Creek Cookery,* with recipes for dishes mentioned in *Cross Creek,* like hush puppies and alligator tail steak. After completing that book, she started another novel, which she called *Sojourner.*

Finally, Norton's year of service was finished, but his health was seriously depleted from a severe form of dysentery. With Marjorie's help, he recovered nicely at Cross Creek, just in time for the unpleasantness of the trial.

Over the years, Marjorie had become acquainted with many prominent writers, Margaret Mitchell, A. J. Cronin, Zora Neale Hurston, and Robert Frost among them. As word of the impending trial spread, Marjorie was encouraged to know that many of them were rooting for her, knowing the trial outcome could affect all writers everywhere. Still, Marjorie felt the personal anguish of being betrayed by someone she considered a friend, although others might have called Zelma a real jerk.

Marjorie's lawyers secured depositions from the publisher, Charles Scribner, from Max Perkins, Henry Canby, from the Book-of-the-Month Club, and military authorities, who offered evidence of the high esteem the armed services had for her work.

As legal costs mounted, everyone knew the lawsuit could surely be settled for much less money than a defense would cost. Marjorie, however, was resolutely against any settlement, for both the personal feeling that Zelma was in the wrong and also because of Marjorie's perception that it was her duty as a writer. Artistic liberty must be protected, and she felt she owed to it all authors.

As she wrote to her lawyer, "What is to happen to all biography and especially autobiography, if a writer cannot tell his own life story, as I did in Cross Creek? And one cannot write his own life story without mentioning, short of libel, others whose paths have crossed his own . . ."

The trial, which began on May 20, 1946, in Gainesville, stirred up a great deal of excitement. The courtroom was packed. Norton was at her side, not only because of his love for her, but because he was named her codefendant, since at that time husbands were jointly liable for civil wrongs of their wives.

Zelma, in her polka-dot dress and high heels, sat nearby, knitting. When she dropped her ball of yarn several times, Norton, ever the gentleman, recovered it for her.

Marjorie, the famous author, wore a plain brown dress and small hat tilted over one eye. She had fifty-five witnesses sworn in, while Zelma, the "aging spinster," had thirteen.

In the opening statements, the prosecution stated that Zelma was enjoying her quiet life until she had to face the undesirable publicity brought on by the malicious description of her in Marjorie Rawlings's novel. Besides the unflattering "ageless spinster" description of her, another passage in the chapter, "Toady-frogs, Lizards, Antses, and Varmints" offended her:

> *My profane friend Zelma, the census taker, said, "The b----s killed the egrets for their plumage, until the egrets gave out. They killed alligators for their hides until the alligators gave out. If the frogs ever give out, the sons of b----s will starve to death."*

The defense stood by the accuracy of the passages, saying Marjorie was writing as a friend, and at the time she thought Zelma would be pleased with the small measure of fame it would bring.

On the second day of the trial Zelma took the stand.

She remained true to her feisty nature, answering questions crisply. To the amazement and amusement of those who knew her, she denied ever in her life taking the Lord's name in vain, but she lost some credibility with many responses, saying she was unable to recall whatever was being asked. Then she faced a formidable opponent.

Marjorie was not only famous, she was witty, down-to-earth, friendly, and intelligent. She disarmed the courtroom, so funny at times that even the judge discreetly hid his face behind his hands. Marjorie convinced everyone listening of her love for Cross Creek, saying her book *Cross Creek* was "a story of my love for the land, and for that particular portion of the land where I have felt that I have belonged, which is Cross Creek. And when you love a person or a place, then their faults and peculiarities—that does not interfere with your love for them at all."

She explained her description of Zelma, the one causing so much trouble, saying she called her a spinster because Zelma "always had admiration from men and opportunities to marry." So, spinster seemed a better word than "old maid." As for Zelma resembling an angry canary, her hair was "golden and she has blue eyes, and she was small and quick," and sometimes angry. As to whether she "should have been a man or a mother," Marjorie thought Zelma had so many abilities, she could have reached great heights had she been a man. And, Marjorie said, she never knew anyone who loved children more than Zelma.

In closing arguments, the defense stressed the rights of writers to freedom of speech. The prosecution emphasized that writers did not have the right to hold up an ordinary citizen for public criticism.

On May 28, 1946, twenty-eight minutes after the jury left the courtroom to deliberate, they returned with a verdict of not guilty.

Less than one month later, Zelma filed a motion for a new trial, citing multiple grounds for error. The motion was denied, but Zelma then appealed to the Florida Supreme Court. In 1948, the Florida high court agreed that Zelma's privacy had been invaded, but fined Marjorie one dollar plus court costs because Zelma had failed to prove she had in any way been injured by the publication of the book.

Friends and legal counsel discouraged Marjorie from filing an appeal. The five years since it all began had taken a toll on her. Her health was fading, and her writing seemed to be going nowhere. Indeed, she never again produced another book of the caliber she expected of herself.

Several years after the unhappy times, Marjorie and Zelma accidentally met in a florist shop and fell into each other's arms. Both said they never wanted to hurt the other one. Zelma claimed it wasn't she who pursued the trials but the lawyers. The two never resumed their close ties, but both were glad for the meeting.

Suffering from a stroke in 1960, Zelma lived her last years in a St. Augustine nursing home until she died in 1963.

When Marjorie died following a cerebral hemorrhage in 1953, her Cross Creek neighbors sent flowers to Norton Baskin with a note enclosed. It read:

Dear Mr. Baskin—
We are sending a list of those who helped in the Flower
arrangements. We all have a very deep regret and a feeling
of looseing someone verry dear to us. I know that your grief
is beyond words, but I can truthfully say that you have
friends and Friends of Miss Rawlings at Cross Creek who
shairs your grief with you. Hope you can stop by with us if
not but a few minutes when you come overhere. We are just
the same as ever.

Friends

CHAPTER 14

Sheriff McCall's Brutal Reign

M ore than one jerk, sometimes many more than one, are often involved in historic happenings. This is true of the events explored in this chapter, but without a doubt one man stands out among all the other jerks. At six feet, one inch, 225 pounds, with size thirteen shoes and huge hands, anyone would stand out, but Willis McCall liked to emphasize his presence by wearing a wide-brimmed Stetson hat and high-heeled cowboy boots on his sizable feet. Also, he consistently displayed an attitude that was hard to ignore. A few moments spent in McCall's presence revealed an ego to match his physique.

He was a Cracker and proud of it. Florida Crackers are descendants of the first white settlers in Florida. The origin of the word "Cracker" is debated, but early Crackers were described as dirt-poor and living in little cracker-box houses, or great consumers of cracked corn, or cow men who were skillful at cracking leather cattle whips.

McCall was born poor in Lake County, Florida, where he and the rest of his family worked their 120-acre farm, often working shoeless in the fields, even in winter. His was a typical Cracker life except, unlike other Crackers, McCall early on decided he would not live his whole life in poverty. At age twenty-one, he married a local young woman named Doris Daley, and they started their family, welcoming three sons in all. He bought some cows to set up his own dairy, installed the first pasteurizing equipment in the county, and named the business the Bluebird Dairy. Working full-time in a grove plus making door-to-door deliveries provided a decent living for the McCalls. The deliveries also afforded him a path to meet people and to work on his "aw-shucks" attitude that charmed even his adversaries.

Five years later, he sold the dairy to become a fruit and vegetable inspector for the United States Department of Agriculture, a position he held for the next nine years. They were years during which the country rebounded from the Great Depression, but the citrus industry didn't just rebound, it roared ahead to overtake California in citrus production. In addition, the new railroads and highways built under President Franklin Roosevelt's relief work programs made shipping citrus faster and easier.

Then, too, the use of DDT during World War II led to its introduction to control destructive insects in citrus groves. All that plus the development of frozen orange juice concentrate further contributed to financial gains in the industry. Lake County was recovering from the Depression along with the rest of the country but was no longer the home of dirt-poor farmers. To be sure, not everyone became a millionaire, but there were many.

As a USDA inspector, McCall forged ties with tycoons of the citrus industry and with bankers and other moneyed men, ties that served him well when he decided to run for sheriff of Lake County. With his folksy demeanor and his chosen trademark, "the People's Candidate," he won the race in 1944, beginning a career that would last for twenty-eight years.

Growing demands for labor in the citrus industry, coupled with so many young men having been drafted into the service, made for an increasing labor shortage in the groves. Florida Governor Millard Caldwell encouraged sheriffs to uphold the "work or fight" laws, which allowed them to keep any fines they collected, up to $7,500 for one year, from loafers or workers who failed to show up for their jobs in the groves. Protests organized against the seven-day workweek resulted in exorbitant fines, and to pay them off, workers were trapped in a situation akin to slavery of the old days.

Sheriff McCall also made use of anti-vagrancy laws. He jailed anyone who protested too vigorously, bullied labor union bosses, and even locked up a union organizer from the CIO (Congress of Industrial Organizations), Eric Axilrod, who had come into town to encourage strikes among workers whose wages had been slashed. McCall jailed Axilrod and then marched him around town in handcuffs before running him out of town.

McCall's anti-union reputation spread, as did his fame as a white supremacist. When World War II ended, black Southern veterans returned home to the same oppression they had endured previously in civilian life. Although they had risked their lives fighting for their country, upon their return they faced poll taxes and literacy tests if they wanted to vote.

A black teacher from Mims, Florida, Harry T. Moore, organized the Florida Progressive Voters League, which was so successful in encouraging blacks to register to vote, it enrolled more than seventy thousand new black voters.

But as things heated up, the Ku Klux Klan held rallies in Lake County to support McCall's reelection, as well as for that of Strom Thurmond's campaign for president. On the night before the election, a motorcade of two hundred Klansmen visited Lake County, followed by a car with smiling Sheriff McCall aboard. Thurmond didn't make it, but McCall won in a landslide. He was unaware that events on the horizon would soon occupy him for years to come.

It all began on a warm July night in 1949, when Norma Padgett, a recently married white seventeen-year-old, claimed she was raped by four black men when she and her husband, Willie, were stuck with car trouble on a country road. Within two hours, three young blacks, Walter Irvin, Samuel Shepherd, and Charles Greenlee were under arrest and a manhunt was on for Ernest Thomas, who by then was almost two hundred miles away.

Mostly, it was presumed that blacks in the Groveland vicinity would operate their own small farms in the off-season to provide for their families, but they were also expected to make themselves available for the chiefly seasonal work in the groves. However, after returning from time spent in the military, both Shepherd and Irvin refused to sign on for grove work. The Shepherd family had farmed so successfully, their farm made grove work unnecessary for them and they became a shining example to others—which annoyed the white community, particularly the sheriff.

On the evening of July 16, childhood friends Irvin and Shepherd, who had served two hitches in the army together, were out for a night on the town thirty-five miles away in Eatonville. It was a bit far for an evening, but Eatonville, the adopted home of the writer Zora Neale Hurston, was the first incorporated African-American town in the United States, and the two friends felt they needed a break from racial bias. Besides, who could resist Club Eaton, a nightclub that featured big names like Ella Fitzgerald, Duke Ellington, and a Florida cat named Ray Charles? They had a fine evening but not a long one, since Irvin needed some sleep because he had promised to work with his father in the morning.

It was past midnight and just a few miles from Groveland when the two veterans, driving Shepherd's brother's car, came upon the Padgetts' Ford stopped by the side of the road. They pulled over and offered to help. Padgett explained he had a dead battery and only needed a push to jump-start the car. Irvin and Shepherd tried, but no amount of pushing worked, and they were soon exhausted and sweating with the effort.

When the Padgetts, both of whom were intoxicated, got out of the car to confer with the perspiring black men, Norma offered Irvin and Shepherd a drink from an opened bottle of whiskey she and Willie had in their car. The two vets gladly accepted, but after they drank, Willie Padgett angrily spat on the ground, saying he'd never drink from that bottle again after they did. It was the last straw for Shepherd. He grabbed Padgett and knocked him out cold and flat into the nearby ditch. He and Irvin got into their car and headed home.

The next morning, Shepherd went to Irvin's house to rehash the night's events. Just as he parked his car, he was startled to see three other cars immediately pull up behind him. Wasting no time, deputies leaped from the other cars and roughly took the friends into custody, beating them mercilessly before hauling them off to the county jail.

Meanwhile, north in Gainesville, sixteen-year-old Charles Greenlee and his friend Ernest Thomas had jobs cooking burgers and washing dishes before they decided to head to Groveland for better paying work in the groves. Greenlee, originally from Baker County in north Florida, and his buddy, Thomas, hitched several rides and then walked the rest of the way, arriving sweaty and dirty at their destination. Thomas was a friend of Shepherd and Irvin, and his mother owned and operated a juke joint in Groveland. He left Greenlee off to wash up at the train station while he started for his home to get clean clothes for both of them.

Outside, as he left the station, Thomas saw a menacing mob forming, could hear the words "nigger" and "string 'em up," and knew it was time to get out. He jumped on the first bus he came to that was heading north. Greenlee never saw him again, and apparently had no idea why his friend split. He learned that later, at a bus stop, Thomas led a posse on a wild chase through jungle-like swamps but was shot dead where he fell asleep, exhausted, in the mud and pine needles, far from Groveland.

The mob and the police, who were bent on arresting four young black men accused of rape by the young, white Mrs. Padgett, captured Greenlee when he ventured away from the station, looking for something to eat. Within a few hours, he met Irvin and Shepherd for the first time in jail.

News of the threat to white supremacy and the untouchable purity of white womanhood roared through the town, and the now enraged mob formed at the county jail, demanding the three blacks be turned over to them. McCall, who was notified of the situation as he was returning from a convention in Ohio, was as aware as anyone that Florida had already recorded more lynchings and more registered members of the Ku Klux Klan than any other state, including Mississippi, Louisiana, and Alabama, the ones usually accorded that dubious record. He knew he had to act.

Determined not to have a lynching on his watch, McCall notified his deputy to move the three prisoners from the jail and to hide them in the woods. When he arrived back at Groveland, he hurried to address the crowd, which by then had grown to two hundred cars carrying five hundred to seven hundred men. Trying to calm them, McCall promised justice would be done. The unruly mob was unconvinced and for days continued to roam through the area, shooting into black homes, setting them on fire, but saving the worst for the Shepherd home, which they totally destroyed. Fortunately, sympathetic whites had removed hundreds of blacks on citrus trucks from Stuckey Still, the black neighborhood just outside Groveland, or the scene almost certainly would have been worse.

As the story spread across the nation, from Oregon to New York City, Sheriff McCall was hailed as a hero for preventing a lynching. In Lake County, his reputation was at stake.

Left with no choice, he finally called for the National Guard. The Guard eventually sent three hundred men, a big help in holding the mob at bay, but in the meantime, the three young men were living a nightmare.

Deputies took Greenlee, the sixteen-year-old boy, to the courthouse basement, where broken glass had been scattered over the dirt floor. They chained him to an overhead pipe, stripped him of his clothes, and beat him with hoses and clubs until he lost consciousness. When he came to, they asked him if he raped the young woman, and when he said, "No," they beat him again and again until he finally said, "Yes," desperate to stop the torture.

Irvin and Shepherd suffered similar treatments, but of the three, Irvin would not confess to the crime, no matter how they beat and bloodied his body.

Meanwhile, Sheriff McCall convinced the mob that the two other prisoners had been already moved to Raiford Prison, although he really had them hidden in the jail until he could smuggle them to a waiting car. Two deputies then sped away with

Irvin and Shepherd handcuffed and lying down in the back of one car. With another car following, the deputies raced toward Raiford Prison, about two hours north, where the prisoners would be held for trial.

On September 2, 1949, intensely interested county residents packed the Lake County Court House. A large fan provided little comfort to the crowd in the ninety-degree heat. Smiling Sheriff McCall resembled a genial host, exchanging small talk with everyone as he milled about among the spectators. A pile of cedar sticks awaited Judge Truman Futch, known as "the Whittlin' Judge," and whittle he did for the entire time the court was in session.

Despite evidence that Greenlee was nineteen miles away at the time of the crime and that Irvin and Shepherd also were nowhere near when the crime was reported to have been committed, it took just ninety minutes for the all-white jury to find the three black defendants guilty. Greenlee, who previously had not known either of the other two defendants, was sentenced to life in prison because of his young age. To no one's surprise, Irvin and Shepherd were sentenced to death.

The three were fast becoming known as the Groveland Boys because of the similarity to the events of an infamous Alabama case when two white women accused nine black men of rape. Those events dragged on for years, becoming well known as the case of the Scottsboro Boys.

Attorneys for the Groveland Boys immediately filed appeals with the Florida Supreme Court. Although the NAACP applied pressure and the *St. Petersburg Times* published a series of credible articles raising serious questions about the crime, the Florida high court upheld the Lake County guilty verdict.

However, less than a year later, in a unanimous decision, the United States Supreme Court overturned the death sentences of Irvin and Shepherd. The justices agreed the convictions did "not meet any civilized conception of due process of law," and they included Sheriff McCall, the state attorney, and the whittling judge in their scathing opinion. They ordered a new trial.

In the evening of November 6, 1951, Deputy Yates accompanied McCall to Raiford Prison to bring the Groveland Boys back to Lake County for their retrial. The two prisoners were handcuffed and sat in the front seat of McCall's car, with Deputy Yates in the backseat. Darkness was descending as they traveled on the deserted country roads when McCall pulled up next to another car parked at the side of the road. There, Yates moved to the other car, which he drove in front of McCall's over the back roads into Lake County. They had gone a few miles when McCall jerked the steering wheel, saying something was wrong with the left front tire. He stopped the car, cursed at his prisoners, and ordered them to get out and fix it.

Still handcuffed to each other, the prisoners were struggling from the car when McCall drew his gun and shot them both. Shepherd was dead, but Irvin was not. He lay motionless on the ground, and later said he heard McCall radio Yates, bragging how the two "tried to jump me and I did a good job."

Although McCall was later officially praised throughout Lake County for his actions, at the United Nations headquarters in New York, the Soviet delegate Andrei Vishinsky shouted to the world that the United States "had a nerve talking about human rights and upbraiding other nations while Negroes were shot down by an officer of the law while in custody."

Even with some new evidence and Thurgood Marshall, future Supreme Court justice, on his side, Irvin's second trial, held in 1952, surprised no one. After deliberating for an hour and a half, another all-white jury returned with a verdict of guilty and recommended the death penalty. As expected, petitions for clemency were denied by Governor Charley Johns. Fortunately for Irvin, Johns lost his bid for reelection, and the new governor, Leroy Collins, commuted the sentence to life imprisonment.

It was no surprise that most of Lake County was incensed, including Judge Futch, the Whittlin' Judge, and Sheriff McCall.

While there existed a widespread belief in the innocence of the two remaining Groveland Boys, particularly outside of

Sheriff McCall and his victims
STATE ARCHIVES OF FLORIDA, FLORIDA MEMORY

the Lake County area, they remained jailed until Greenlee was paroled in 1960. Understandably, he left Florida, married, and raised a family in Tennessee, where he opened a successful small business.

When Irvin was paroled in 1968, he moved to Miami to live with a sister. As a result of the severe wounds he received at the hands of McCall and Yates, his health never returned to normal, but he was able to work in construction. He received permission to return to Lake County for a family funeral in 1969. Shortly after his arrival, he was found in a car, appearing to be asleep, but actually he was dead of natural causes, according to the Lake County Sheriff's Department. Justice Thurgood Marshall was not the only one with doubts about the cause of death listed on the Lake County report.

Virgil McCall continued to do what he could to prevent his beloved state of Florida from changing from his version of a "lawanorder" (always pronounced as one word) state to a leftist one dominated by the NAACP and the United Nations. It took a court order in 1971 to prompt him finally to remove the WHITE and COLORED signs from waiting room areas in his jail.

In 1954, McCall involved himself in a segregation case, which was called the Platt case. The family of Allen Platt, descendants of Croatan Indians, moved to Florida from South Carolina. When the five children started attending a white school, as they had always done before their move, some classmates mentioned their somewhat darker skin at home. Sheriff McCall was notified and visited the Platt home and rudely examined and photographed them, initiating action to have them removed from the white school. Their landlord asked them to move because of threats that their house would be burned. Although the Platts won the decision in a resulting court case, it couldn't have been much comfort for the family.

Countless other examples of Sheriff McCall's ugly conduct exist, but a particular one unarguably qualifies him to join Florida's other jerks, as if more were needed.

In 1972, Tommy J. Vickers, a black Miami truck driver who was charged with a twenty-six-dollar auto inspection sticker violation, crossed McCall's sense of self-importance in the jail. McCall ordered three prisoner trustees to put Vickers down on the floor. When they did, Vickers resisted—a bad move. Seven days later, he was hospitalized and died from "acute peritonitis resulting from a blunt injury to the abdomen."

Although McCall swore he had only put a foot on Vickers's arm when he started to struggle, then "reached over and gave him some pops," when questioned under oath, the trustees testified that the sheriff had kicked the prisoner's abdomen several times when he was down. McCall was indicted, suspended from office, and brought to trial, just as he was campaigning for reelection.

Unfazed, he worked crossword puzzles, napped, and read during his trial. Seventy minutes after the all-white jury deliberated, they returned with an acquittal and McCall resumed his up-to-then charmed life.

The charm was gone now, though. Florida was changing, and many Floridians were changing. McCall lost his election and retired to his ranch, where he spent much time perusing the scrapbooks he had made over the years. They were filled with news clippings of his career, even the less-flattering ones. He died in 1994 at the age of eighty-four.

CHAPTER 15

KKK: Organized Jerks

Jerks are everywhere, and certainly Florida has always had her share. Not only did the Sunshine State become home to many individual jerks, it unofficially rolled out the welcome mat for a whole organization of jerks. Actually, the group originated in Pulaski, Tennessee, and was formed after the Civil War by six veterans of the Confederacy. They claimed their purpose was to "have fun, make mischief, and play pranks on the public."

All in their twenties, James Crowe, Calvin Jones, John Kennedy, John Lester, Frank McCord, and Richard Reed had served the Confederate cause honorably, some having been wounded or imprisoned. They were looking for relaxation and diversion in their surroundings where, understandably, the defeated townspeople were brooding and sullen. The veterans decided they themselves would have to take on the responsibility for their recreation.

They formed what was nothing more than a hilarious social club, they said. They named themselves Ku Klux, a corruption of the Greek word *kuklos,* which meant "circle," then added clan, spelled with a *k* for consistency.

In homemade, ghostlike finery sewn by their wives, they paraded around town at night, playing what they referred to as their "boyish pranks." Unfortunately, from the beginning, their pranks were foisted almost entirely on black people.

In addition, with the readmission of Confederate states into the Union and the Reconstruction agenda of forgiveness and the acceptance of a ban on slavery, many former Confederates had become more determined than ever to perpetuate the racial divide. When the Freedmen's Bureau, which had been set up to assist ex-slaves, was reauthorized in 1866, not totally unexpectedly, racial violence broke out all over the South, with Florida being no exception.

Florida Klan rally and cross burning
STATE ARCHIVES OF FLORIDA, FLORIDA MEMORY

Several days of violence, first in Memphis, then in New Orleans, left many blacks dead and wounded before the violence in Florida escalated to a point where the federal government was forced to order local governments to suspend operations in five counties. The Klan thus felt a need to reinvent itself, changing from an organization that pulled pranks to one of vigilante operations.

By 1867, the Klan regarded itself as a defender of the hallowed white, Southern way of life. It divided itself as follows: Each of its "realms" (states) was to be ruled by a grand dragon and eight hydras; every "dominion" (congressional district) by a grand titan and six furies; every province (county) by a grand giant and four goblins; every local "den" by a grand cyclops and two night hawks, the den being made up of rank-and-file ghouls. A grand wizard and ten genii would oversee the empire.

Choosing to travel incognito, the Klan entered Florida masquerading as part of the Constitutional League of Florida, which was a group pledged to support the US government, to counteract evil influences on the nation's politics, and elect officials who would support their aims, but whose prime purpose was to "oppose Negro Suffrage and all those who favor it."

As expected, when Florida was readmitted into the Union in 1868, racist events escalated. The federal army was recalled, and Congress ratified the Fourteenth Amendment to protect the freedmen from having their rights invalidated. In just six days, five freedmen were murdered, and sadly, it was only the start of blacks being murdered for little or no reason.

In November 1868, the Florida Klan outdid themselves with a clever exploit. A sizable number of muskets that had been purchased by Governor Reed to be used by the state militia were en route by train at night from Jacksonville to Tallahassee. Federal troops serving as guards on the train did not notice when Klan members boarded the train at a stopover. The Klansmen worked silently and quickly, throwing the muskets out of the two cars. They then hopped off the train at the next stop and made their way back along the tracks, retrieving the guns along the way.

Jackson County was a leader in Florida's unacknowledged race war at a time when freedmen who owned land were marked by the Klan, many of them slaughtered in a short time. Blacks were not the only Klan targets, however. Catholics and Jews shared that dubious distinction. One longtime Jewish store owner in Marianna, Samuel Fleishman, became the Florida Klan's first Jewish fatality when a group of Klansmen entered his store, took all the guns and ammunition he had for sale, and then marched him out onto the highway, where they shot and killed him.

Although Jackson County led the list in Klan violence, Alachua County was a close rival. It was there that five men were put on trial for the murder of nineteen blacks, and all were acquitted by juries made up of Conservatives, the new name adopted by former Confederates. Columbia County came next, with sixteen black murders in three years, and then Hamilton County, with ten within the same time period, all credited to the KKK.

Freedmen who had the audacity to purchase parcels of land raised the ire of the Klan and became targets for night riders. Blacks who tried to buy land were frequently flat out refused, but if their offer was accepted, after they paid their money they were terrorized into deserting their newly purchased land by night riders.

The Klan has never provided any records of their members, but scores of prominent people were definitely known to be numbered among them, including one nine-term legislator, legions of Confederate officers, a distinguished law professor, an associate justice of the Florida Supreme Court, wealthy merchants and landowners, and countless lawmen.

The Democratic press of Florida generally denied that the Klan existed in the state, even going so far as to denounce any attempts to prosecute white criminals. Not only did local law authorities avoid investigating racial crime, some of them joined in the brutality. Nor were politicians above the monstrous goings-on. Governor Fleming praised the Klan, publicly describing several lynchings in such detail that it sounded very much like an eyewitness description. Though their names were not on any membership list, many Florida bluebloods joined the KKK or were fiscal supporters of the organization.

Additionally, the Tallahassee press was controlled by Democrats, and both the *Weekly Floridian* and the *Tallahassee Courier* unequivocally stated that the Klan did not exist in Florida. They were joined in their opinion by the *Marianna Courier*.

Florida totally ended any gains blacks made during Reconstruction by establishing a poll tax in 1889, the first state to do so, effectively curbing black votes and ending the gains they had already made. Racists triumphed, Jim Crow flourished, Klansmen were idols. One noted Princeton professor who would become president of the United States, Woodrow Wilson, proclaimed the "great Ku Klux Klan, an 'Invisible Empire of the south,' bound together in loose organization to protect the southern country from some of the ugliest hazards of a time of revolution." The popular Florida Governor Napoleon Broward urged Congress to buy land in Africa in order to establish a colony for blacks. Governor Sidney Catts, the white supremacist discussed in another chapter, gratefully accepted the support of the KKK.

On January 8, 1915, an event that would lead to a resurgence of the Klan took place in Los Angeles, but the effects spread nationwide. D. W. Griffith produced a movie, *The Birth of a Nation,* which glorified members of the Ku Klux Klan as saviors of the white race. The movie impressed viewers as being a documentary, leading Floridians, like the rest of the country, to believe what they saw in the film was fact. At a private White House viewing, now President Woodrow Wilson declared, "It is like writing history with lightning." He further stated, ". . . my only regret is that it is so terribly true." While the film was received almost reverentially in the South, predictably, Northerners were not in agreement about it.

However, in the 1920s, the Klan was enjoying a spread in membership throughout the USA. It was estimated to have from three to five million members nationwide, with approximately sixty thousand in Florida.

It was during this time period that Warren G. Harding succeeded Woodrow Wilson in office, and rumors swirled that Harding became a Klansman during his term. It has never been proven, but through the years, the story persisted that a five-man Imperial Induction Team joined the president in the Green Room of the White House to perform the ceremony. It has been reported that the team was so nervous, they forgot to bring their Bible with them from their car, so Harding had to use the White House Bible.

The tale goes on that in appreciation, Harding gave War Department license tags to each team member, which would allow them to go through red lights anywhere in the country.

Considering that Harding gave a high priority for supporting civil rights, the story seems most unlikely, but it will not die.

In the 1920s, Florida held "Klan Days" in schools when robed knights presented high school students with flags and Bibles. Klansmen also offered their "protection" at beaches, picnics, fairs, and other outdoor functions, always insisting that the purpose of their organization was to honor white women and preserve white supremacy. They could never bring themselves to accept black suffrage.

As the 1920 Election Day approached, violent racial clashes multiplied. One of the deadliest episodes took place in Ocoee, a tiny town of three hundred citizens near Orlando, where one black man's attempt to vote inspired a white mob to rampage for a week and ended with between thirty-five and sixty-five dead. Whites also burned a church, a school, and eighteen homes, but when NAACP officials petitioned the attorney general to investigate the Klan's involvement, the request came to nothing. Surviving blacks left their homes and belongings behind when they escaped to safety.

Following episodes of bombings, beatings, and tar and feathering, the Klan passed around fliers stating: "EVERY NEGRO who approaches a polling place next Tuesday will be a marked man." The treacherousness multiplied, reaching from the Panhandle to Jacksonville to Key West.

From the beginning, the Klan claimed that it had assumed the responsibility of defending "the sanctity of the home and the chastity of womanhood." Carrying out this pledge would lead to the worst civil rights violation in Florida history on January 1, 1923, when an entire black town was eradicated.

The town of Rosewood, in Levy County, was situated three miles from Sumner, an all-white town on a road that led to Cedar Key, a few miles out in the Gulf. Blacks made up the majority of Rosewood's hardworking families and the two towns coexisted without problems for years. Rosewood did well with its cedar and turpentine mills, a school, a general store, and a Negro League baseball team—well enough to inspire rancor among some whites in surrounding areas, but mostly without serious problems. That is, there were no serious problems until New Year's morning 1923, a very cold morning.

On that morning, while her husband, James, was at work at the Cummer and Sons sawmill, Fannie Taylor, a white mother of two who was found near her home, battered and bleeding, claimed she had been assaulted by a black man. James returned to find neighbors caring for Fannie and the children and crowds of men gathering.

Her story was accepted with no questions asked and instantaneously assumed to be true. Actually, the pieces of her story were disjointed and not entirely credible, but the mob that was forming began its charge down the road, attacking any blacks who were unfortunate enough to be in the vicinity, even shooting an aged grandmother.

Meanwhile, bloodhounds joined the search of the neighborhood while James begged for help from Alachua County, where the KKK had been celebrating, rallying, and contesting justice for blacks as they marched through downtown Gainesville. Responding to Taylor's plea, some four to five hundred Klansmen, infuriated and armed, descended on Rosewood, where a tale was spread that a black man, Jesse Hunter, had recently escaped from a road gang. Although there was no proof that he had attacked Fannie Taylor, the posse needed none. They began systematically killing blacks in Rosewood and burning their homes, in the process destroying any evidence as to what had actually occurred. With help from some sympathetic whites, Rosewood residents who did escape ran into the woods, and none ever returned.

Rosewood was gone. The number of deaths was never determined, estimates varying from eight to close to a hundred. It took three weeks before Governor Hardee ordered an investigation begun. Then, after a month, the special prosecutor found insufficient evidence to bring charges, and no arrests were made. It would be seventy years before the state of Florida would recognize the tragic atrocity and provide monetary compensation to relatives of Rosewood's victims.

Blacks were not the only ones targeted by the Klan. Nativism, the defense of white America, at various times inspired the barring of Irish Catholics, then Asians, Italians, Slavs, and Russian Jews from American shores. The Florida Klan particularly focused on Greeks, many of whom settled near Tampa. Jews, branded as vermin or worse, were always a prime target and superseded only by Catholics, who topped the list. The Klan was, of course, unhappy when Catholic Al Smith was chosen to run for president on the Democratic ballot. Florida joined with four other former Confederate states to favor a Republican president in the 1928 election, much to the pleasure of the KKK, which was gradually losing members in the Northern states.

Herbert Hoover won the election, but confidence in him and in the Republican party evaporated quickly on Black Tuesday in 1929. The Klan had initially favored Franklin D. Roosevelt in 1932, but his support for and from blacks, Catholics, and Jews soon ended that. Klansmen added radical labor unions and communists to their list of enemies. The abolition of the poll tax in 1938 was a devastating event for the KKK, but it also was a reminder for members of their duty to eradicate black voting.

During World War II, over a half million blacks served their country and rightfully expected a better life when they returned home. However, it was not to be, for only nine days after V-J Day, a policeman beat and drowned a black farmer. Madison County was the scene of a lynching one month later, which aroused a schoolteacher and NAACP officer, Harry T. Moore, to action.

Moore was a black educator/activist, married to Harriette, also a teacher. He was taking sample ballots into his classrooms to teach his ninth grade classes about voting—at a time when voting was a lily-white privilege. In his free hours, he organized the

NAACP in Brevard County, recruited members nonstop, and filed a suit for equal pay for black and white teachers. He gave speeches, wrote letters, and passed out fliers, attempting to arouse protests concerning unequal salaries, segregated schools, and disproportionate funding for black schools. In 1944, he moved his focus to police brutality and lynching after the two post–V-J Day fatalities in Florida. His reputation was spreading. It was a dangerous move, but from then on, he investigated every lynching in Florida.

Representing the NAACP, Moore kept up an unrestrained battle with Sheriff McCall (who earned his place as the subject of another chapter in this book), in which Moore called for the sheriff to be suspended and indicted for the murder of the Groveland Four defendants. McCall was never indicted, but because of Moore, newspapers all over the country carried the story.

At the time, Moore was working without NAACP salary and putting in long hours. In a disagreement with some members of the organization, he also was pushing hard against raising members' dues, as he was certain so many members could not afford it, and many members would be lost because of it.

It turned out that Moore was right. After he had almost singlehandedly increased membership to over ten thousand in Florida, only three thousand remained after dues were increased.

On Christmas Day 1951, the Moores had gathered with their family to quietly celebrate both the holiday and their twenty-fifth wedding anniversary in their home, a few miles from where a large group of Klansmen were enjoying a barbecue. Moore's mother had come from Jacksonville, and their daughter, Peaches, had traveled from Ocala where, like her mother, she taught school. Evangeline, their other daughter, was to join them the following day when she came from her job at the US Department of Labor in Washington, DC.

They spent most of the day at the home of Harriette's mother, who lived nearby, along with Harriette's brothers, Arnold and George, who were home on leave after an overseas tour of duty with the army.

Back in their own home, while Peaches and Moore's mother retired, Harriette and Moore reminisced and shared a special anniversary cake before they, too, went to bed at about 10:00. At 10:20 a bomb exploded beneath their bedroom floor.

Awakened by Peaches's screams, Harriette's brothers tore from their mother's home, piled the injured couple in George's car, and headed to a hospital, but it was too late for Harry. He died on the way, and his wife died nine days later.

The tragic bombing of the home of the known civil rights leader set off a furor of a level that had not been seen for some time. The *New York Times* led prominent newspapers and news magazines in condemning the crime, while Governor Warren was openly criticized throughout the country for not having done more to prevent such lawlessness. Vacationers canceled plans to vacation in the Sunshine State, and the United States was condemned for its racism in the United Nations General Assembly.

The investigation conducted by the FBI was subsequently termed a sham and a farce by the press. Then in February 1952, a grand jury convened to hear testimony in the Moore murders. Testifying for the Ku Klux Klan were thirty Klansmen, but while the grand jury placed the blame for the crime on the Klan, the identity of the actual murderers was still unknown. Although some Klansmen were indicted for perjury, the murders of the first civil rights martyr and his wife have never been solved.

There had been massive resistance to desegregation in the classroom as required by the US Supreme Court in 1954. This was true in Florida as in the rest of the states below the Mason-Dixon line, but times were changing, and while the Klan was losing members, other white supremacist groups sprouted. Though they might deny any connection to the KKK, their goals were similar, as one Klan grand dragon declared the KKK to be "against integration, communism and federal controls."

An increase in Klan activity during the 1960s coincided with the time of Martin Luther King–inspired demonstrations, restaurant sit-ins, and school integrations. With the passing of the Civil

Rights Act, signed by President Lyndon B. Johnson in 1964, the equal protection of citizens was increasingly enforced. In 1965, the president signed the Voting Rights Act, further ensuring the voting rights of all citizens.

Around that same time, the House Committee on Un-American Activity (HUAC) used ridicule against the KKK, causing membership in the Klan to decline drastically. By the 1970s, the roll was estimated to be just five thousand.

In 1978, Edward L. Spivey, a seventy-year-old professed Klansman, admitted to an FBI agent that he had been present at the scene when the murders of Harriette and Harry Moore took place but stated that his friend, another Klansman, Joseph N. Cox, was the one who carried it out.

When the agent reviewed the old records, he learned that in interviews with Cox in 1952, FBI agents had informed him they had strong evidence against him. Following the last interview with him, Cox had killed himself with a shotgun blast to the head, leaving no suicide note and, according to his family, having never shown any suicidal tendencies.

Another Klansman with a reputation for violence, Earl J. Brooklyn, had a floor plan of the Moores' home in his possession and had enlisted volunteers to assist him in some unspecified job, including his Klansman friend, Tillman H. Belvin.

The four men are all dead, and the case has never been officially solved, but the publicity it inspired seemed to have influenced a number of its more prominent members to abandon the Klan, leaving it with a membership mostly from a lower social and educational status than had previously been recruited.

Since then, the Klan has devoted their energies toward other moralistic issues. *Roe v. Wade* inspired terrorism against abortion clinics, since, the Klan said, all abortion doctors were Jews. In an advertisement denouncing gays and lesbians in *Thunderbolt,* the Klan's Atlanta newspaper, a longtime Klansman praised God for AIDS, a disease which he claimed would eliminate those undesirables.

The Klan rolls swelled, then declined, and swelled again, but still they endured. Splinter groups broke off and changed their names but fostered the same beliefs and practices. One can only imagine how the elections of 2008 and 2012 must have affected Klansmen who still profess,

Yesterday, Today, Forever,
Since Eighteen Hundred and Sixty-Six,
The KU KLUX KLAN
has been riding and will
continue to do so as long as
the WHITE MAN LIVETH.

CHAPTER 16

McCarthyism Invades Florida

At the start of the Cold War, United States Senator Joseph McCarthy launched his search for communists in our government wherever he could find them. Likewise, Florida Senator Charley Johns and his committee used the threat of Communism, the so-called "Red Menace," as a cover to investigate and eliminate civil rights organizations in Florida, particularly the NAACP.

The booming population in the southern part of Florida following World War II threatened the prevailing influence of the conservatives in the more sparsely settled north. Johns was a member of the Pork Chop Gang, twenty staunchly conservative legislators from northern Florida. They qualified as twenty jerks, determined to stop integration and to preserve the political and financial power they enjoyed despite the scattered lesser population of their rural counties as compared to counties that were home to the cities of Tampa, Jacksonville, and Orlando.

Before his election to the Florida Senate, Charley Johns, a native of the state, worked as an insurance agent and as a railroad conductor. A product of Florida public schools, he attended the University of Florida for only a few months and left before he earned his degree. He was elected to the State Senate in 1947, assumed the position of senate president in 1953, and then became acting governor when Governor Dan McCarty died a few months later, after serving just eight months of his term. As governor, Johns promptly removed many government officials, mostly McCarty appointees, from their jobs in order to install his own conservative associates.

Although he was generally liked by most of his colleagues, some never hesitated to reveal Johns's lack of formal education. Even so, during his brief time in office, he did push for progress in state highway construction and for prison reform. He also presided at the opening of the Sunshine Skyway Bridge across Tampa Bay in 1954. However, after failing to be reelected for a full term, he returned to the Senate, where he was still able to wield considerable clout. He served there until 1966.

Following the Supreme Court's 1954 unanimous *Brown vs. Board of Education of Topeka* decision, pronouncing segregation in schools violated the equal protection stipulation in the Fourteenth Amendment, segregationists were staggered by the resulting issues that began to crop up. Pork Choppers were particularly incensed, insisting that *Brown* was a violation of states' rights.

The University of Florida Law School was ordered to immediately admit Virgil Hawkins, a black public relations director at Bethune-Cookman College, who had first applied to UF in 1949. About the same time, two Florida A&M coeds instigated a bus boycott in Tallahassee, which set off an even bigger protest movement in the city, while another bus boycott got off the ground in Miami, with guidance from the NAACP.

While Senator McCarthy's fishing expedition for communists was going on in 1956, Johns went on record with the statement that there was "no doubt that communist people were behind all of this racial agitation." He proposed a bill that would create a committee to investigate the actions of communists and those promoting integration, specifically the NAACP. The bill passed nearly unanimously in the Senate and overwhelmingly in the House, enabling the Pork Choppers to use "McCarthyism" to rout the NAACP, stop integration, and maintain their accustomed control over the state.

They called their group the Florida Legislative Investigation Committee. Along with Johns, prominent among the committee of jerks were the chief investigator, R. J. Strickland, of Tallahassee; and from Tampa, attorney Mark Hawes, a graduate of the University of Florida Law School. For the next nine years, the committee would humiliate, terrorize, and otherwise intimidate professors and students, forcing them to reveal their formerly private lives. One committee member did ask if his 1930s membership in the KKK would prohibit his association with the committee, but Johns said he didn't think it would make a difference.

It was a time when many Americans suspected the Soviets eventually wanted to overthrow this country. These people believed African Americans were a group that would most likely fall for subversive propaganda, with the result that they might assist the Soviets. The American Communist Party did connect with African Americans in the 1930s when they defended the "Scottsboro Boys," and the party also sided with them when they challenged unfair employment practices. However, at their 41st Convention, the NAACP decided to investigate possible communist infiltration into their group and to expel any of their branches that might show the slightest connection.

The Florida Legislative Investigation Committee, otherwise known as the "Johns Committee" because of its chairman, started off aggressively with the NAACP in its sightline. They badly wanted to strangle the NAACP, which they believed would slow down and hopefully even put an end to integration, a prime concern of theirs. To begin with, the FLIC suggested that the NAACP lawyers were guilty of barratry, which is legalese for repeatedly bringing lawsuits for the sole purpose of harassment. The committee suggested that not only had they incited the lawsuits, perhaps they even financed them.

Anticipating legal troubles, the NAACP headquarters wisely asked the Florida chapters to collect all of their bank and other records, pack them securely, and send them to the New York offices for safekeeping.

Attorney Hawes called Virgil Hawkins to Tallahassee, determined to trick him into testifying before the Johns Committee that he had received funds from the NAACP for his campaign to enter the University of Florida law school. Hawes also wanted to prove the direct involvement of Thurgood Marshall, Roy Wilkins, and the NAACP, but he failed utterly on both counts.

In fact, the Tallahassee investigations revealed no working ties between Communism and the NAACP or to any other African-American organization.

However, another state committee had been studying tuberculosis hospitals, and while investigating the hospital staff, that committee accidentally learned there were homosexuals in the group. In the process, they also came upon names of teachers and school authorities who were suspected homosexuals. Coincidentally, Senator Johns's son told his father about rumors concerning some on the UF faculty whom students thought "acted gay." And so, the hunt was on.

Meanwhile, the FLIC chief investigator, Remus Strickland, was operating mostly undercover in order to evade any media and avoid unfavorable publicity. Using FLIC funds, Strickland paid students to inform on classmates. He telephoned professors in the wee hours, ordering them to his motel room to provide information. Conversations were secretly taped.

The Johns Committee demanded records from the university health center workers and confiscated some clinical records. Gay faculty and students were permitted to remain at UF only if they agreed to receive psychiatric therapy while on campus. The committee confiscated medical records, including some from unmarried female students who had delivered babies.

Still hoping to incriminate the NAACP as being a communist cover, the FLIC probed for communist connections at Florida State University and at FAMU (Florida Agricultural and Mechanical University), again with no startling results. Then, an announcement from the University of Florida faculty council declaring immediate integration motivated the Johns Committee to move on to the University of Florida at Gainesville.

The shift came at the same time as the two years were up that had originally been stipulated for ending the FLIC's existence, unless some reason deemed it necessary to renew it for another two years. As committee chairman, Johns was expected to give a report to the legislature, and he faced having to admit publicly that his committee had detected no collusion between communists and the NAACP or the university. Undaunted, Johns succeeded in having the committee's life extended for another two years in

Senator Johns planning to screen undesirables
STATE ARCHIVES OF FLORIDA, FLORIDA MEMORY

order to conduct a search for much easier marks—homosexuals and other "subversives"—even though the FLIC actually lacked constitutional authority to conduct such a search.Nevertheless, Strickland got things rolling by having the chair of the Geography Department at UF and a leading scholar, Sigmund Diettrich, brought to the Manor Motel for questioning. Diettrich later told a colleague that after an hour and a half, he knew "they were through with me and my life work was in a shambles." Soon after the interview, the professor was fired from the position he loved; shortly thereafter, he attempted suicide.

During the time the Johns Committee operated at the University of Florida, they successfully pressured the university to fire twenty members of the staff and faculty and to expel over fifty students. The American Association of University Professors and the American Association of University Women did not sit idly by. Both organizations were outspoken in their defense of their fellow professors. The AAUP advised their members about their rights, but there was great concern among the faculty that their private lives could be exposed in the media, and some feared the consequences should they seek to challenge the committee.

The FLIC headed on to Tampa, ready to take on the new school there. Things were different in Tampa. The brand-new University of South Florida was located in the city, unlike the more rural settings for the other universities, and USF's creation had been opposed by the rural Pork Choppers who refused to concede any power to the city Lamb Choppers, the representatives of the more progressive city dwellers. It was a well-known fact that the faculty of the trailblazer school openly discussed such topics as atheism, racial equality, and even Communism in classes. In addition, USF was an integrated university in a segregated state.

The Johns Committee went to work, promptly castigating the faculty for discussing or featuring speakers sympathetic to Communism or evolution. They learned instructors went so far as to assign "obscene" books such as *The Catcher in the Rye,* which the committee labeled "intellectual garbage."

From the beginning, the president of the university, John Allen, had been excited and proud of his brilliant faculty and of his new young school, where he believed everything was open for discussion and all beliefs could be talked about without fear. Then came the Johns Committee and its search for communists, homosexuals, integrationists, or any other subversives.

Investigator Strickland and attorney Hawes set up their operation in a Tampa hotel room, where they had police haul faculty and students from their classrooms to question them for hours about purported homosexual encounters, dubious reading matter, and subversive pressures. When President Allen learned of their procedures, he insisted that they at least had to move their investigations from the motel room to the university campus.

At first, the committee focused on one instructor, Thomas Wenner, who had criticized the conservative John Birch Society—a newly formed anti-Communism organization—in his class. The Birchers labeled him a communist and called for his resignation. Wenner was suspended until he finally changed his classroom practices, and the committee moved on to other faculty members.

Sheldon Grebstein was the assistant professor of English at the University of Kentucky for nine years before moving to Florida, enticed as others had been by the prospect of a new university with great potential and unbound by traditions. In his class, he discussed an article containing some mild profanity by a well-known neoconservative, Norman Podhoretz, which Grebstein had used in his Kentucky classes. Unfortunately, the article fell into Charley Johns's hands; Grebstein was soon suspended and censured for circulating offensive handouts to his students. After a very unpleasant and protracted showdown, he moved out of Florida, saying, "The greatest boost that higher education could get in this state would be for the Johns Committee to be put out of business."

Another professor, John W. Caldwell, resigned after being investigated. He minced no words, saying, "These police state methods have made me and my colleagues almost physically ill, and I cannot tell you the contempt I feel as a result."

The committee played a role in rescinding the acceptance to USF of another professor, based on his being a member of a communist group. However, the real communist member was another man who had the same name except for his middle initial. The wronged professor had already moved his home and belongings to Tampa but no longer had a job in Tampa.

As unrest among the faculty grew, much of the student body, which had come to USF expecting innovative teaching, was also greatly concerned. The student government enthusiastically and loudly advocated academic freedom. An anonymously composed song, written to the tune of "Santa Claus is Comin' to Town," made its way around the campus. The first chorus was:

You better watch out,
You better not cry,
You better be good,
I'm telling you why,
Charley Johns is coming to town.

Most of the students and much of the faculty, it seemed, were incensed. More than half of the 2,500 students signed a petition declaring their objection to the presence of the FLIC on their campus. Then, too, newspapers had begun to publicize and criticize the methods used by the committee.

The Johns Committee attorney, Mark Hawes, spent two hours giving the committee's latest report to the State Senate, during which he blasted USF as being immoral, irreligious, and tolerant of sexual freaks.

University of South Florida president John Allen was truly between a rock and a hard place. He wanted first and foremost to protect the visionary university, but crossing the FLIC might possibly cause the state legislature to deny critical funds.

A week after Hawes's report, Allen received permission to take his turn before the state legislature, an unusual proceeding. Allen called Hawes's testimony "a skillful blend of truths, half-truths, and omissions." He spent just twenty-five minutes talking, but in that time he eloquently defended his school from Hawes's allegations, then defined academic freedom by stating unequivocally: "A college is not engaged in making ideas safe for students. It is engaged in making students safe for ideas." The Florida legislature gave Allen a standing ovation.

Having produced a report of several thousand pages, the Johns Committee complimented USF on its "beginnings of a great university" but still cautioned those in authority to be ever vigilant for signs of moral lapses.

Even so, the Johns Committee was not quite ready to fold. They switched their area of concentration to public school teachers. These efforts resulted in teachers being grilled behind closed doors, sometimes being fired or having their licenses invalidated.

The investigators' methods relied on intimidation and fear. They removed teachers from their classrooms and then questioned them in front of other school administrators and without legal counsel or being told why they were being questioned. Teachers were questioned about friends and romantic connections, with the unspoken threat of possible public exposure.

It was becoming increasingly clear that the Johns Committee's importance had begun to decline, undoubtedly somewhat affected by the passage of the Civil Rights Act in 1964, which was accompanied by a lessening of threats from segregationists.

After functioning for nine years, the Florida Legislative Investigation Committee nevertheless attempted to finish its work with a flourish. In the spring of 1964, they published their report, "Homosexuality and Citizenship in Florida," which they distributed to state officials and to the media. Commonly known as the Purple Pamphlet, both for the color of its cover and for its subject matter, the booklet alienated many of the committee's former supporters, even Pork Choppers. It contained graphic photographs and a glossary of terms shocking to many Floridians but which caused it to become popular reading material. It sold for two dollars in New York City, and then went nationwide.

Just as Senator Joseph McCarthy had claimed to have a list of communists in the State Department but was proved to be lying, so too did one committee member swear he knew of 123 homosexuals in Florida educational institutions. He also was later proved to be lying.

The already controversial committee became even more so, and the time came when its funding would soon expire. The FLIC faced facts and shut down. To spare Johns and his committee humiliation, the legislature sealed the records of the FLIC and ordered them to remain sealed until 2028. However, with the enactment of a state constitutional amendment directing the opening of most legislative records in 1992, more than twenty-five thousand pages of records revealed the threatening methods and the hiring of informers that had been used on hundreds of law-abiding Floridians. The names of informers and witnesses were blacked out, but other names remained.

The records were alarmingly revealing. A political science professor at UF came under suspicion because he and his wife entertained integrated parties at their home. Another report labeled a professor "one of the worst pinks if not actually a member of the Communist Party in the University of Florida." Students became subversive suspects because they read such suspicious material as John Steinbeck's *Grapes of Wrath* or the works of J. D. Salinger. Being too cozy with members of the NAACP or being seen anywhere near places where homosexuals socialized made a person suspect. Furthermore, those who testified before the committee were reminded that perjury could result in prison sentences of as much as twenty-five years.

Altogether, the Johns Committee was responsible for untold numbers of students dropping out of college, for professors and public schoolteachers losing their jobs, and for the unknown aftermath that had to have followed it all.

Until the end of his life, R. J. Strickland remained proud of his investigative work with the Johns Committee. He bragged to anyone interested that he was pleased with the service he did, especially for the children.

Charley Johns never backed away from the work of his committee, and never expressed doubts about the "good" he and his group had done. More than once, he stated that if he and his committee had saved even one boy from life as a homosexual, it had been worth it. Johns died in 1990.

Undoubtedly, some prospective students were discouraged from attending Florida universities when they heard about the antics of the Johns Committee, and certainly highly qualified professors must have turned away to other schools. Hopefully, the reputation of the committee and the accounts of its actions will be so abhorrent that Florida will never again overlook, even for a little while, the intrusion of any committee or lawmakers of any status into the freedoms of their citizens.

CHAPTER 17

Justice for Adam

It is hard to believe that as recently as 1981, while the National Crime Information Center kept files on cars, boats, and race-horses, it did not accept data on missing children. Milk cartons had no photographs of children's faces; there were no Amber Alerts; there was no Missing Children's Act and no pedophile registry; and parents didn't worry about their children playing outside where they couldn't see them. It took the kidnapping and murder of a little Florida boy and the fierce determination of his grieving parents who, for twenty-seven years, never stopped looking for the monstrous jerk who ended his life.

Actually, jerk is too kind a word to describe this fiend, monster, savage, freak, degenerate being. No word is adequate to describe the beast who kidnapped, murdered, and dismembered Adam Walsh, an innocent child. And it is hard to believe that anything good could follow such a heinous act, but it was because of that despicable crime that the National Center for Missing and Exploited Children was created, the Missing Children's Act became law, and national child abduction alerts came into being. Perhaps these aids would eventually have been enacted in any case, but how many children might have lost their lives or been terrorized or tortured in the meantime? One would have been too many.

It was a scorching morning on Monday, July 27, 1981. The temperature was predicted to reach the nineties, not unusual for the middle of summer in Hollywood, an east coast Florida city of about 120,000. It would be a normal summer day in the Walsh household.

John Walsh was off to his job as director of marketing for the Paradise Grand Hotels in Bal Harbour. Revé Walsh completed her usual morning chores while six-year-old Adam watched *Sesame Street*. Revé dressed for her one o'clock gym time and laid out clothes for Adam— green shorts, a red-and-white-striped polo shirt, sneakers, and his favorite, a too-big beige nautical captain's hat that he loved. She would drop off his next year's tuition check at St. Mark's school office, stop at the nearby mall to check Sears for some brass lamps she and John had been wanting, and then take Adam over to Gram's for a visit while she went to the gym for her workout. As they were leaving, she noticed that Adam had skipped the sneakers she put out for him in favor of his yellow flip-flops—a real Florida boy.

It was a short ride from St. Mark's to the mall, where they walked hand in hand across the parking lot into the Sears entrance they always used. The toy department was the first section inside past the catalog desk, the lamp department next beyond toys and to the left. But in the center of all the toys, Adam spotted a video display of computer games, which were new and exciting at the time.

Revé hesitated a moment when he begged to be allowed to stay and watch the few boys who were playing the games, but since it was so close to where she would be, she gave in, telling him she would be back in a few minutes and would only be a few aisles away in the lamp department. She pointed it out to him and he said, "Okay, Mommy. I know where that is."

They were the last words she would ever hear her son speak.

It couldn't have taken longer than seven minutes for Revé to learn the lamps she wanted had not come in and to leave her name and phone number for the store to call her when they did. She headed straight back to the toy department, noticing as she did that the blare of rockets and blast of gunfire at the video display had stopped. The children who had been playing were gone too. Adam was gone.

She looked about her, panic rising. She called his name. No answer. He had to be close by. Outwardly maintaining self-control, she asked clerks and customers in the area if they had seen a little boy in a captain's hat. The store was not crowded due to the summer slump, but no one had seen him.

Icy fear grew inside her as she kept searching, and she finally located a young security guard named Kathy Shaffer. Revé showed her the photo of Adam she kept in her wallet, one in which he was wearing the same shirt he had on that morning and his big grin showed his missing upper right incisor and the new tooth poking through his gum. When she told the guard he had been missing for forty-five minutes, Shaffer had Adam paged over the store's PA system. The store kept repeating the announcement every fifteen minutes, but after frantically searching the aisles and calling his name for two agonizing hours, Revé notified the Hollywood Police Department, located directly across Hollywood Boulevard from the mall. She then called John, who dropped everything, bulldozed his way through traffic, parked his car, and tore into the mall.

Together, they gave gathering police officers more photos of Adam and all the pertinent information they could think of before John made a quick trip home and returned with a blanket and pillow to make a bed in the backseat of Revé's car.

They kept questioning everyone they saw, but the store was rapidly emptying of customers and no one had seen Adam. Fighting panic and terror, they left some of his toys and books in the car, with a note telling him to stay in the car and that they were looking for him. Leaving Revé's car unlocked, they headed home in John's car as lights in the mall stores were going dark.

They did not know—fortunately—what was in store for them or how many years their agonizing torment would go on. They had no idea that the local police would make one mistake after another or that the FBI would refuse to get involved without evidence that the case was not strictly a local matter. The Hollywood Police Department tried to convince the Walshes that Adam had probably wandered away and would turn up as most children do eventually.

While their frustration with the local police grew with each passing day, the Walshes were grateful to friends, relatives, and neighbors who notified radio stations to broadcast alerts over the air. Off-duty police officers offered help, some truck drivers took off work to search, and ordinary people were walking, bicycling, driving through the streets, searching dumpsters and canals, looking and calling for Adam.

When he had been missing for forty-eight hours, the HPD finally reached the conclusion that possibly Adam had not simply wandered off and could have been abducted. It was what Revé and John believed from the start, knowing Adam was not a child who would wander away. Someone must have taken him, they were convinced, perhaps someone who had recently lost a child or someone who could never have children.

While the search continued, friends of John's made up and started passing out 150,000 posters with a photo of Adam taken a week before, grinning widely to show his missing tooth. Included was an offer of a five-thousand-dollar reward and a promise not to prosecute anyone who would safely return Adam.

Two agonizing weeks had passed before some local fishermen made a gruesome discovery. They found a severed head floating in a canal west of Vero Beach and turned it over to Indian River County homicide detectives. Because Revé and John were out of town, a good friend of John's made the short trip to Vero Beach and positively identified it as Adam Walsh's head.

The Walshes had been cooperating with investigators, including undergoing polygraph tests, which proved conclusively that they were not involved in Adam's disappearance, but they did everything they could think of to help find whoever was responsible for the abduction of their boy. They were in New York City being interviewed about their missing son on *Good Morning America* when they received the devastating news that the head in the canal was Adam's. They knew then they would never have their precious son back. Clinging to each other in their grief, they became even more determined to find whoever took him from them.

Back in Florida, well-meaning people who wanted to help seemed to fill the Walsh home with chaos all day, every day. When Revé and John finally fell into bed totally exhausted, they would sleep for an hour or two, then awaken to the horror that their lives had become. They held on to each other, weeping together.

It was not until four days after Adam's disappearance that police interviewed Kathy Shaffer, the seventeen-year-old security guard at Sears, who recalled an incident that had occurred that day at the video display in the toy department. She remembered two white boys and two black boys were there arguing, getting a bit loud before she told them they had to leave. She put the black boys out the north door and the white boys out the west door. Having studied the photo of Adam they showed her, she thought he might have been the smaller white boy but was uncertain. John and Revé knew if Adam had been put out the west door, he would have been totally confused, because the north door was the only one the family ever used.

Concerning what happened next, words were not needed. Both knew it must have been where Adam's terror began.

On August 15, 1981, a Mass of the Angels, the Catholic funeral service for children younger than seven, was held in Hollywood, attracting more than a thousand people to honor Adam.

As devastated, broken-hearted, and physically exhausted as Revé and John were, they knew they couldn't rest. They had to pursue every possibility, learn all they could, do everything they could to find Adam's killer.

Eight weeks after his death, on October 6, 1981, at the request of Congressman Paul Simon and Senator Paula Hawkins, John and Revé testified before Congress about the need for a Missing Children's Act. They learned it was estimated that over 150,000 children went missing every year, and of those, possibly 50,000 were victims of stranger abductions. John felt some pride in being able to report that as a result of an appearance he made on *Good Morning America,* three of the children whose photos had been shown on the program were found. Publicity was important, he stressed, and nothing surpassed television for getting the stories with photos out quickly.

Meanwhile, Revé resolved to put to work some of the thousands of dollars that people contributed along with more than fifty thousand letters of sympathy they received. She determined to work full-time for missing children, which was how the Adam Walsh Outreach Center was born. After she announced it to local

The Walshes watch Governor Graham sign missing children's bill.

newspapers, donations of equipment along with an offer of the use of an office poured in. Relatives and friends donated time toward the stated goals of first, helping to get the Missing Children's Act passed into law; second, helping police find missing children; and third, offering a hundred-thousand-dollar reward to anyone who successfully helped to identify Adam's killer.

Somehow, the Walshes made time for trips to New York for a second appearance on *Good Morning America* and to Chicago for the *Donahue* show. They participated as consultants for a TV movie entitled *Adam,* which was shown and then rebroadcast twice; each time, more missing children were located. A sequel, *Adam: His Song Continues,* produced similar results. The films were credited with finding sixty-five children, the best thing to happen in a long time. Additionally, John began hosting the television show *America's Most Wanted,* which resulted in countless incidents of captured criminals.

It was rewarding to see the results of the publicity, but Revé and John lived every day and every night knowing that Adam's murderer had still not been brought to justice. They were haunted by thoughts of Adam's last moments, agonizing over how much he might have suffered—and for how long? The thoughts were unbearable. They couldn't sleep. They couldn't eat. Both were losing weight, looking almost as bad as they felt.

In the meantime, in Jacksonville, a degenerate by the name of Ottis Toole came to the attention of the authorities. He was a man with a low IQ, putrid breath, filthy clothes, rotten teeth, and a despicable attitude. First arrested at age seventeen, he was arrested nearly every year after that for charges ranging from vagrancy and prowling to lewd behavior, making obscene phone calls, and public intoxication. That history was bad enough, but he moved on to setting fires. When he was arrested for arson in 1983, he confessed to setting thirty-six houses on fire over a period of twenty years. He was sentenced to fifteen years for one fire and five years for another, with his sentences set to run consecutively in the Florida State Prison at Raiford.

While Toole was imprisoned at Raiford, his former companion, Henry Lee Lucas, was arrested and imprisoned for murder in Oklahoma. Not only did Lucas admit to murdering one woman, he told Oklahoma authorities he had murdered more than two hundred others and said he had been helped with some of the crimes by an old partner, a Jacksonville man: Ottis Toole.

When notified, Florida authorities interviewed Toole, who freely confessed to committing at least sixty-five murders or helping a buddy commit them. But then, the air of nonchalance he had about him as he talked about the murders gave way to a sense of nervousness the detective hadn't seen before as Toole went on to admit murdering a young boy on one of his travels in the South. He said it was a boy he found in a Broward County Sears store, and Toole became visibly upset when he told how he cut off the boy's head, tossed it behind the front seat of his Cadillac, then cut up the rest of the body and threw the pieces away. He drove another five or ten minutes before he saw a canal, where he stopped and threw the head into the canal. Then he drove to the next plaza, where he cleaned the blood off himself in the gas station. He repeated more than once that it was the only killing that he ever felt sorry for.

Gradually, he related how he had driven to south Florida intending to find a child he could take home to raise for his own. He saw the white boy outside a Sears store, he said, and told the kid he had toys and candy the kid could have if he got in his car. The little guy did, but when Toole started to drive away, the boy started crying and wanted to get out of the car, angering Toole so much he hit the child's face to shut him up. He struck the boy between the eyes, and then punched his stomach and the boy stopped crying.

That was it, he said. That was how it happened, and he felt bad about it now.

Jacksonville police immediately notified the Hollywood authorities, but there the pace slowed. Hollywood police issued a statement that Ottis Toole, already convicted of two other murders, would be officially charged with the abduction and murder of Adam Walsh the following day.

Unfortunately, it didn't happen the following day. Or the one after that, or the next one either. The Walshes generously tried to make excuses for the HPD, saying they were busy, they were doing the best they could, and besides, Toole retracted his confessions more than once, almost as soon as he made them. But all the while, the bereaved parents seethed and howled inside. Even after John received a despicable, obscene ransom letter from Toole, which he showed to the HPD, the lead detective on the case remained unconvinced as to Toole's guilt.

Meanwhile, the Walshes continued their lives as best as they could. In 1982, they brought a baby girl into the world and named her Meghan; in 1984, her brother Callahan was born. Another son, Hayden, joined their family in 1994, but the couple never stopped aching for their first-born son.

With John as host, the early ratings of the television program *America's Most Wanted* were remarkable and grew impressively. Not only was it popular with viewers, but from the very first program, criminals were caught because their photos were broadcast along with an 800 number that made notifying authorities simple. As soon as the first criminal face appeared on the screen, calls started coming in; a few days later, the first one was caught. The program was off to a remarkable beginning. John felt some satisfaction to be partly responsible for putting some criminals in jail.

Despite the excellent ratings, and for reasons known only to them, network officials ordered *AMW* replaced in 1996. It was a shock John didn't understand. A show that had helped bring home twenty kids, helped capture over four hundred dangerous criminals, including eleven of the FBI's most wanted, was canceled? Nevertheless, John decided to make the last show, which would be the 427th one, the one closest to his heart. The story of Adam's disappearance together with an announcement that it would be the final show opened the floodgates. Protests poured in, making such an impression that *America's Most Wanted* was off the air for just six weeks.

However, unknown to the Walshes, the health of their son's imprisoned murderer was steadily going downhill. Always a heavy drinker and drug user, Toole was diagnosed with advanced cirrhosis of the liver, essentially untreatable. Physicians transferred him to the Lake Butler Prison Hospital, where he intermittently prayed and raved about the many bad things he had done in his life and especially begged God for forgiveness for killing little Adam Walsh. Fittingly, he died alone and was buried on the prison grounds.

The disappointment the Walshes felt about their son's killer never having been convicted of the murder was compounded when they learned of Toole's death. They could never have their son back, they knew, but they wanted justice. They wanted his killer convicted.

Twenty-five years after Adam's murder, Revé and John decided they would wait no longer for closure. They had to know beyond a shadow of a doubt that their son's killer had been caught. They contacted an old acquaintance, a retired Miami Beach police detective, Joe Matthews, who agreed to take on their very cold case.

Conducting a meticulous review of the enormous piles of records and files, Matthews made some startling observations. He interviewed a Mrs. Arlene Mayer, who said that two days before Adam was abducted, she had reported to the HPD that Toole had accosted her daughter at a Hollywood Kmart and disappeared when her daughter screamed and made a scene. Mrs. Mayer had identified Toole by his photograph at HPD, but nothing was done. Would Adam still be alive if HPD had investigated?

Matthews also interviewed the young female security guard who told him although she couldn't identify Adam as being one of the boys she escorted out the Sears door that day from the first photo they had shown her, when they showed her another, she knew it was Adam. She was just seventeen, she said, and so afraid of what would happen to her that she lied.

Matthews went on to learn that the old Cadillac that Toole had driven was eventually junked, as was the carpet from the car, which had to have been bloodstained, and which would have helped in the investigation. Files also indicated that five rolls of film were taken by the Florida Department of Law Enforcement, mostly of Toole's car, but when Matthews requested copies of the photos, to his incredulity he learned they were never developed. He requested they be developed and copies sent to him.

Among the photos taken were specialized ones using a technology that illuminated items containing blood residue that might not appear visible to the naked eye. Matthews studied them carefully. Among the pictures taken of the Cadillac floorboards behind the front seat was one that turned his blood cold. It could be nothing else but the bloody imprint of a boy's face. Toole stated he had tossed Adam's head there. Matthews knew he needed to show the photo to Adam's parents, painful as it would be for them.

As soon as they saw it, they knew. They clung to each other. They knew. Their search for Adam's killer was over.

On December 16, 2008, the Hollywood police chief, Chad Wagner, called for a press conference attended by reporters from all leading media sources. After he apologized for the errors of the HPD to the Walshes, Wagner stated absolutely that Ottis Toole was the abductor and murderer of Adam Walsh, and had he still been alive, he would indeed have paid for his crime. Instead, as the result of grievous investigative oversights, the ultimate jerk in Florida's history died without ever having spent a single day in court for his horrific actions.

CHAPTER 18

Even Heroes Can Be Jerks

It was July 24, 1999. The ground at Florida's Kennedy Space Center trembled beneath the feet of the eight women whose eyes remained glued to the sky as the Space Shuttle *Columbia,* under the command of Air Force Lieutenant Colonel Eileen Collins, blasted through NASA's glass ceiling, shattering it at long last as the shuttle roared over Cape Canaveral. The women, invited guests of Collins, held their breath, and with clenched fists, they watched the fiery exhaust trail until it disappeared into space.

The first US woman in space, Sally Ride, had served as a crew member aboard the *Challenger* on June 18, 1983, an interminable twenty years and two days after the Russians sent up Valentine Tereshkova, but it had taken thirty-six years before NASA permitted a woman to command a shuttle.

Collins believed that her guests on the ground, Jerrie Cobb, Janey Hart, Wally Funk, Jerrie Sloan Truhill, Sarah Gorelick Ratlet, Irene Leverton, Bernice Stedman, and Rhea Hurrie Woltman, the Mercury Thirteen women who were able to make the trip to Florida, were the ones who made it possible for US women to be astronauts and consequently made it possible for her to be the first female shuttle commander. They belonged to the Mercury Thirteen, thirteen talented and determined women who had passed the same battery of tests at the illustrious Lovelace Foundation as the Mercury Seven astronauts did, but were banished by the boys club at NASA and the US government. Collins, who had been the first woman pilot of a shuttle in 1995, made a point of inviting the women to each of her liftoffs. It was time to say thank you, she said.

What became known as the race for space began on October 4, 1957, with the launch of Russia's first satellite, *Sputnik,* an object twenty-three inches in diameter and weighing only 184 pounds.

Seven of the Mercury Thirteen
NASA

But the shock of it awakened the sleepy nation to the panicky realization that the US was in second place in space. It was no small thing for the country representing Communism to win a symbolic battle in the Cold War.

Convinced there was no time to waste, in 1958, President Eisenhower signed the National Aeronautics and Space Act, establishing the National Aeronautics and Space Administration (NASA), whose purpose was to acquire the scientific knowledge necessary for space flight. The organization was to be under civilian control.

Dr. Randolph Lovelace, chairman of NASA's Life Sciences Committee, teamed up with Air Force Brigadier General Donald Flickinger to create a medical testing program for astronaut aspirants to be carried out at the Lovelace Clinic in Albuquerque and at the Aeromedical Laboratory at Wright-Patterson Air Force Base in Ohio. They were arduous tests, taken and passed by all seven of the white, middle-class, Protestant, crew-cut men who, when their identities became known, were immediately hailed as heroes, to be forevermore known as the Mercury Seven. They were Alan Shepard, Gus Grissom, John Glenn, Scott Carpenter, Wally Shirra, Gordon Cooper, and Deke Slayton. The public wanted to know everything about them, and the media was eager to supply the facts about the nation's newest celebrities.

What was not yet known was that for several sound reasons, Lovelace and Flickinger were seriously considering the practicality of sending a woman into space.

Their first consideration was that since the female body is smaller and lighter, there would be less fuel required to lift the rocket into space, and continuing throughout the flight, females would use less oxygen. Secondly, it was a fact that women had fewer heart attacks than men, which could be important under stressful changes in gravity. Third, since female reproductive organs were internal, it was believed that they would be less affected by radiation, and finally, in legitimate tests, women surpassed men performing in cramped spaces or in isolation.

Flickinger had developed an Air Force–affiliated plan to test women for space flight, which he wanted to call the Women in Space Program. But when he consulted with NASA about including women in their tests, NASA turned him down.

Jacqueline Cochran, who at that point in time was the most famous woman in aviation, was a personal friend of Lovelace and his wife. Cochran had set countless records in speed, altitude, and distance. During World War II, she founded and was the director of the Women's Airforce Service Pilots (WASP), whose function was to free up male pilots for combat flights by having women fly military planes to locations where they were needed. Considered to be arrogant and competitive by people who knew her, Cochran promoted women in aviation, but only if those she promoted recognized that she was in first place. Never a shrinking violet, she wrote two autobiographies, one not-so-subtly titled *The Autobiography of the Greatest Woman Pilot in Aviation History.*

Born Bessie Pittman in 1906 to a dirt-poor family in the Florida Panhandle, she would later falsely claim to have been orphaned. Later, she helped to support her family members financially for years but never publicly admitted they existed. When she was eight years old, she worked a twelve-hour shift in a cotton mill and at eleven, confidently apprenticed herself to a hairdresser to learn the trade. She was a teenager when she married, delivered a baby boy three months later, divorced, and grieved when the baby died in a house fire. She moved alone to New York City when she was nineteen years old, then moved to and worked in Pensacola, where frequent dates with pilots from the Pensacola Navy Base fostered her interest in flying. She then spent some time in Philadelphia before moving back to New York City.

When she exited the train at Grand Central Station in New York, she was no longer Bessie Pittman. She had decided to assume the more striking name of Jacqueline Cochran. Never lacking in confidence, she applied and was accepted for a job in the famous Antoine's beauty salon in Saks Fifth Avenue department store, which included working in Antoine's salon in Miami Beach in winter months. The fabulous hotels, private boats, tennis clubs, and conspicuous wealth of the tropical paradise impressed Cochran. She knew it was the kind of life she wanted.

During one stay in Miami, she met Floyd Odlum, a married millionaire industrialist, one of the richest men in the United States, who had begun life as a son of an itinerate preacher, poor, much as she had been, and as determined to achieve success as she was. When they met, his marriage was at a point where it plainly was over, and he felt that Cochran was his soul mate, despite her cocky and seemingly selfish egotism.

While they spent the next four years committed to each other, but not married, Cochran took up flying with a vengeance, winning races and, before long, setting records. Seven months after Odlum and his wife divorced in 1935, he and Cochran married. From the earliest days of their marriage, he encouraged and generously supported her participation in air racing, a very expensive hobby.

The next years were busy ones for both of them. Cochran continued to win races, set records, and collect honors. When Amelia Earhart disappeared, Cochran had no qualms about assuming Earhart's role as America's chief woman pilot. Cochran further sealed her importance during World War II by ferrying military aircraft, then organizing and heading the WASPs, and by intimidating military elite, politicians, and anyone else who got in her way.

Odlum continued to make money, lots of money. During this time, he assumed a position as chairman of the board of directors for the Lovelace Foundation, a position he held for twenty years.

Late in 1959, though rejected by NASA, Lovelace and Flickinger were both still interested in establishing a program to test women for space flight. At an Air Force Association meeting in Miami, they met a young woman, Jerrie Cobb, who seemed to fill the bill as a perfect candidate. They knew Cobb was a young licensed private and commercial pilot who delivered bombers and fighter planes, and, like Cochran, she had set records for speed, altitude, and distance.

Lovelace and Flickinger, aware that the Russians were planning to send a woman into space, invited Cobb to become the first one to take the test in their program. Cobb agreed, but when the Air Force learned about the program, concern about growing unfavorable publicity convinced them they wanted to be involved in no part of a plan to test women. Nevertheless, Lovelace made up his mind to take over the plan privately at his clinic, with his friend Floyd Odlum agreeing to finance it. Cochran was past the age limit for the program and had developed some health problems that disqualified her from any active participation, but Odlum insisted his wife must be a leader in it. She could not imagine how anything having to do with women and flying could not involve her in some important, preferably high-profile capacity.

Admittedly, Cochran was unaccustomed to taking a backseat when it came to anything related to women and flying; but on the other hand, she also intensely disliked the women's movement despite the fact that it promoted women as aviators. She never liked to compete with women, preferring to set records in men's competitive events.

It was February 1960, a time when only 25 percent of women had jobs, when they were not permitted to serve in the military, and when no woman could take out a bank loan or buy large household appliances or property without permission from her husband. As she entered the laboratory building in Albuquerque, Cobb knew that if she failed in the upcoming tests, she would almost surely never get another chance and probably no other woman would, either.

For the next six days, she resolutely endured seventy-five tests that included having her ears and extremities nearly frozen, having various nerves subjected to electrical charges, swallowing three feet of rubber hose, submitting to physical endurance tests on a stationary weighted bicycle, nightly barium enemas, and nine hours in a sensory deprivation tank, which was hours longer than any of the men had lasted. Along with countless blood, stool, and urine tests, Cobb endured eye exams, a gastric analysis, a colon exam, a painful ear test for equilibrium, and on and on.

Cobb, the first woman to pass the same tests as the men had taken, inspired the press to go all out when the news about her became public. Nearly every article about her described her as pretty, listed her measurements, and mentioned how she loved high heels.

After completing the testing at the Lovelace Foundation, Cobb headed for the Oklahoma City Veterans Hospital, where a psychiatrist was administering sensory deprivation experiments that had interested Lovelace and Flickinger. After three days of psychological and neurological tests, Cobb allowed herself to be immersed in a soundproof isolation tank filled with water that was kept at body temperature. The expected time limit of tolerance was about six hours, but Cobb lasted nine hours and forty minutes before technicians decided to end the test.

For the sake of comparison, the men who were said to have been similarly tested had been placed in a dark, soundproof room for two to three hours. John Glenn sat at a desk writing poetry when he took his test.

Determined to do all she could to prove women should be included in the space program, Cobb agreed to Lovelace's arrangement to go on to the Naval School of Aviation Medicine in Pensacola, Florida, for spaceflight simulation testing. As part of her increased presence on the scene, Cobb also helped to line up twelve other women pilots she knew or knew of, who were eager to join the program.

Of the twenty women who applied, twelve besides Cobb were chosen. They were Rhea Hurrle Allison, Myrtle T. Cagle, twin sisters Jan and Marion Dietrich, Mary Wallace Funk, Sara Gorlick, Jane Hart, Jean F. Hixon, Irene Leverton, Jerri Sloan, Gene Nora Stumbough, and Bernice Trimble Steadman.

From the beginning, Cochran could not hide her resentment of Cobb's becoming the recognizable face of the Woman in Space Program.

That Odlum was financing it made it even less palatable to Cochran. Added to that annoyance, she learned, too, that James Webb, NASA Administrator, had appointed Cobb to be a special consultant to NASA. Not only did Cochran's husband inform Lovelace of her displeasure, Cochran herself informed the deputy chief of Naval Operations in Pensacola about her concerns about the Woman in Space Program. He, in turn, contacted NASA and was told they had not officially requested the program. The Women in Space Program was ended right then, thanks largely to a hero/jerk named Cochran. The women who were expecting to be tested were informed that candidates for testing had to be military jet pilots with engineering degrees. No women were jet pilots because the military did not accept or train women to be jet pilots, so that ended it.

Not only were the twelve women disappointed when they were notified, some had even lost their jobs because their bosses would not give them the time off for the tests, and, in their eagerness to be included, they had resigned rather than miss out on the exciting opportunity.

Cobb, feeling she had to take it upon herself to do something drastic about the cancellation, began contacting sources in Washington and at NASA. Disregarding that she had been the featured speaker at the NASA-sponsored First Woman's Space Symposium, NASA canceled her role as their consultant.

However, one of the twelve women in the Women in Space group was Janey Hart, wife of a US senator, who, through her connections, was able to arrange a meeting with Vice President Lyndon Johnson. Unfortunately, that accomplished nothing but more frustration. In fact, unknown to them, Johnson, too, exhibited some jerk-like behavior by sending a letter to NASA concerning women in the space program that said, "Let's Stop This Now!"

Undaunted, Hart wrote to both Senate and House subcommittees on space asking them to call meetings for the purpose of determining whether or not women were being discriminated against in the space programs. The Senate would not respond, but the House Committee on Science and Astronautics agreed to take it up and hold a meeting in July with New York Congressman Victor Anfuso, the chairman of an eleven-member group that included two women.

Although Jackie Cochran avoided Jerrie Cobb, she did talk things over with Janey Hart over a lunch. Cochran, as usual, knew she was right, stating that the scheduled program was inadequate and the women should begin again with a larger program and with more women participating, all of which Janey knew would take much longer to produce results, and would require more funds when twelve qualified women were ready to go. Women should not complicate the men's program, Cochran said, and put forth the opposite of all the arguments she herself had used when she was establishing the WASPs. Hart left convinced that Cochran felt if she could not be the first woman in space, she could not stand to see any other woman do it either. As it turned out, others were sure Hart was not wrong about that.

Jerrie Cobb flew to Washington to speak to the subcommittee, along with Janey Hart. Each side of the question was scheduled to have two speakers, but when Cochran arrived unannounced, she prevailed on a committee member she knew personally and received his permission to speak. NASA had scheduled George Low, a director in the Office of Manned Space Flight, and astronaut John Glenn to represent them, but when Cochran was given the go-ahead, NASA, in fairness, added astronaut Scott Carpenter to their side.

Cobb was first to speak. Answering an immediate question as to why the other women in the program were not present, she said first of all, no funds had been provided and some could not afford the trip, but secondly, they had not been invited. Cobb outlined brief but impressive biographies of the other women, emphasizing their notable qualifications: an owner and operator of her own air service, a former WASP and Air Force Reserve captain, a university flight instructor, a civilian flight instructor for the Georgia Air Force Base, and on and on.

She added facts about women's body weight being less than men's, along with their ability to withstand isolation, pain, and extreme temperatures, and then closed eloquently, passing the floor on to Janey Hart, wife of a senator and mother of eight children.

Hart, a passionate speaker, reminded listeners how much talent was wasted when women were made to wait their turn at so many things, refuting the idea that women be refused to take part in space exploration because there was no manpower shortage and they were not needed as the WASPs had been during World War II. "It is not unwomanly to be intelligent, to be courageous, to be energetic, to be anxious to contribute to human knowledge," she said.

When one committee member argued that women couldn't become astronauts because none were qualified to be jet pilots,

Cobb replied piloting in space was not like flying jet airplanes, but rather equivalent flying experience was more important. Actually, four of the women in the Loveland space program had more flight hours than any of the Mercury Seven men. The questions and answers continued until Jackie Cochran made her entrance.

She was introduced by the committee chairman as "the foremost woman pilot in the world . . . who holds more national and international speed, distance, and altitude records than any other living person."

Cochran reminded all about her experience in World War II before she continued, saying that she did not believe there had been any discrimination against women in the astronaut program thus far. She stressed her opinion that since there was no shortage of qualified men to serve as astronauts, work on a program specifically for women could slow down the entire schedule. Point by point, she offered what she thought should be done.

First, she asserted that many more women should be included, organized, and begun on a well-structured program. She added that it would help to eliminate problems of attrition among the women because of marriage and childbirth, which could be costly. Not known then was the fact that John Glenn would make his exit from the space program just two years later and Scott Carpenter a few years after that.

Cobb and Hart could feel their blood pressure rising as the day's hearings ended.

Excitement accompanied the next morning with the presentations by heroes Glenn and Carpenter and by George Low.

Low offered that since time and equipment were limited, NASA had to limit its use to the astronauts already in the program. Upon hearing this comment, Cobb was probably not the only one who mumbled that there seemed to be enough time and equipment to train chimpanzees, but evidently not enough to train women. It was rather like schoolgirls only being allowed to use the gym after the boys were finished.

Carpenter spoke after Low, offering his opinion that since space exploration was so uncharted, much of the dangers should be solved before others could join. In other words, one committeeman observed, men must protect women and keep the field for men.

When John Glenn had the floor, he made a statement he probably regretted for a very long time. He said, "The fact that women are not in this field is a fact of our social order. It may be undesirable."

Glenn was apparently unaware of the emotions his statement inspired. He seemed to be saying to Cobb and Hart and the other women pilots that people should accept things the way they are. To Janey Hart, his statement indicated a refusal to fight wrongs. Slavery had been a fact of our social order at one time, too, she later reminded everyone.

Cobb and Hart were further distressed when the chairman gaveled the hearings to an end. They had been told there would be a third day, but the chairman announced that enough evidence had been presented, and although he offered to accept further written statements for the record, he believed another day of actual hearings was unnecessary and would be a waste of time.

The women could hardly believe what had just happened. But one thing couldn't be more plain: Whatever favorable impact their testimony had been having, it all went up in smoke when Cochran uttered her first statement.

Cobb and Cochran were the only two women who submitted a written statement to the committee. Included in Cobb's was all her medical information favorably comparing her results with the men's from both the Lovelace studies and from Pensacola.

Cochran's statement was a reminder that there had never been a program for women in space authorized by NASA, and incidentally insinuated that Cobb should not be considered a proper speaker for the group.

Three months after the hearings were completed, the House Committee on Science and Astronautics issued its report, stating, "After hearing witnesses, both Government and non-Government, including astronauts Glenn and Carpenter, the subcommittee concluded that NASA's program of selection was basically sound and properly directed, that the highest possible standards should continue to be maintained, and that sometime in the future consideration should be given to maintaining a program of research to determine the advantages to be gained by using women as astronauts."

There was no shortage of jerks, it seemed.

Cobb was discouraged, but she continued to press her case until 1965, when she at last decided her talents could be better used. She flew food and medicine to the destitute people in the Amazon jungle, earning little money, but more importantly, she was nominated for the Nobel Peace Prize in 1980.

At a suggestion from Betty Friedan, Hart channeled what energy she could spare from raising her big family into helping to found and actively working for the National Organization for Women.

Cochran, the girl from the Florida Panhandle who grew up to be one of the most famous woman pilots in the world, died in 1980, still nursing some bitterness that she had never made it into space.

CHAPTER 19

Queen of Florida Jerks

Most of the jerks discussed in this book are men, but the female serial killer who is the subject of this chapter will more than make up for that imbalance. Judias Buenoano entered the history books when she became the first woman ever electrocuted in the state of Florida and only the second one executed in the state's history.

People who know all the facts generally agree that while Buenoano unquestionably deserved her fate, the story of the first woman put to death in Florida tends to arouse sympathy. She was known only as Celia and was the mixed-race slave of Jacob Bryan, a white farmer in the Jacksonville area. Records have been lost since the crime took place on December 7, 1847, but it seems that not only was he Celia's father and master, Bryan was also believed to be the father of Celia's four children.

We don't know what finally set Celia off, but while working in the fields one winter morning, she decided she had enough. When Bryan attempted to discipline her, she beat him with her hoe handle and then slashed his head with a huge heavy knife, killing him instantly. Convicted by a jury, Celia was condemned to die by hanging. After her execution on September 22, 1848, Celia's body was disgracefully permitted to dangle for an hour.

Celia was known by one name, but Florida's second woman to be executed had many names. Claiming a Latina background, she was born Judias Anna Lou Welty in Quana, Texas. She was called Judias or sometimes Judi, but eventually became known as the Black Widow.

For years she claimed her mother, Judias Mary Lou Northam, was a full-blooded Apache and that Geronimo was her great, great grandfather, both claims later totally disproved. Judi was two years old in 1945 when her mother died of tuberculosis and her

Judias Buenoano

MELISSA SIMS/THE PALM BEACH POST

father sent her and her baby brother, Robert, to live with grand-parents while two older siblings were put up for adoption. When Judi was twelve years old, her father married again and brought her and her brother back to join him, his new wife, and her chil-dren in Roswell, New Mexico.

Unfortunately, it was not a happy combined family. According to Judi, she and Robert were both badly abused by their father and stepmother. Both claimed they were forced to work almost as slaves, burned with cigarettes, beaten, and starved. Judi endured the cruelty for two years, but one day when their stepmother began beating Robert, Judi cracked. She grabbed a pan of hot grease from the stove, spattered it on her two stepbrothers, and then tore into her stepmother with both fists. She hurled what-ever she could reach at either her stepmother or her father before they could subdue her. Although she spent sixty days in jail among drunks and the lowest criminals, when she had the opportunity to return home, she refused. She chose instead a girls' reformatory, the Foothills High School, in Albuquerque, New Mexico, where she remained until she graduated in 1959.

By then, she was finished with her family, including Robert. She wanted nothing to do with any of them ever again, but she did return to Roswell, where she worked as a nurses' aide, using the name Anna Schultz. In 1960, she gave birth to a son, whose father was rumored to be Air Force Sergeant Art Schultz, sta-tioned at a neighboring Air Force base, but Judi would not confirm that. Although she never married the father, she named her son Michael Schultz.

Less than a year later, using the name Ann Schultz, she did marry another Air Force man, James Edgar Goodyear. After the birth of their son, whom they named James, Goodyear adopted Michael. A daughter, Kimberly, rounded out their family one year later.

Upon completion of his one-year tour of duty in Vietnam, Good-year was assigned to McCoy Air Force Base in Orlando, where the rest of the family joined him. Their combined finances enabled Judi to open the Conway Acres Child Care Center.

It was shortly after his return from duty in South Vietnam that Goodyear began to complain of not feeling well, and of extreme fatigue and decreased appetite, then nausea, vomiting, chills, and fever. When the symptoms progressed to an onset of jaundice and tingling hands and feet, he was admitted to the naval hospital in Orlando. His condition continued to deteriorate while medics frantically tried to get to the bottom of his illness, but on September 16, 1971, Goodyear was dead. Five days later, the widow collected on his three life insurance policies, which amounted to ninety thousand dollars.

More trouble followed before the year was over when Judi's home caught fire, resulting in another ninety thousand dollars in insurance being paid to her. She quickly rebounded, however, and in 1972, moved her family to Pensacola, where she found work as a nurses' aide at the Escambia County Nursing Home. She met Bobby Joe Morris, a swimming pool construction company employee, and before very long, she, her children, and Bobby Joe moved in together.

However, it seemed to be a relationship of convenience, certainly not the romance of the century. When Bobby Joe took a job as a water purification specialist for the city of Trinidad, Colorado, he went alone. Not until six months later did Judi and her children follow. She and Bobby Joe bought a house together, and although there was no wedding, she adopted the name Mrs. Judias Morris and started to attend a nursing school.

Within months after Judi arrived in Colorado, Bobby Joe, who had always been the picture of health, collapsed at the dinner table and had to be rushed by ambulance to San Rafael Hospital. Doctors ran tests, but were unable to find any reason for his sudden illness. Consequently, as he began to recover, they sent him home, to be watched over by his LPN wife. At least, that was what she claimed to be. There are no records of her completing any education other than high school.

Bobby Joe's condition continued to improve under Judi's care. Every day, she brought big cans of Hawaiian Punch for him, a treat she said he loved. Although still without a diagnosis, he seemed to be making progress. Then suddenly, mysteriously, after a week at home, Bobby Joe Morris was dead.

Judi quickly moved to have his body cremated, but before she was able to complete the arrangements, Bobby Joe's mother managed to have it returned to the family's hometown in Alabama. In spite of his family's interference, Judi collected on three of Bobby Joe's life insurance policies. Her finances were beginning to add up.

She decided it was time for some changes in her life, and one of the several she made was to revert back to the name Goodyear, but this time, she used the Spanish equivalent, Buenoano, for herself and for the three children. Another change was to move back to Pensacola, where she bought a two-story home for her young family on Whisper Pine Drive in Gulf Breeze, Florida. She also purchased a new Lincoln Town Car to transport the four of them to Pensacola in style, all of which was in spite of the fact that her earnings as a nurses' aide were just $3.05 an hour at that time.

The worst was yet to come. The next target was her first-born son, Michael, who had been a problem of sorts ever since he was a small child. Along with his below-average IQ, weak hearing, and bad eyesight, he was also a bed-wetter and a poor student. A difficult child, he needed intermittent psychiatric care over the years. He dropped out of high school in his sophomore year, but was able to make enough progress that he was accepted when he joined the army in 1979. He made it through basic training at Fort Leonard Wood in Missouri.

Although Judi must have known that when Bobby Joe had worked for the city of Trinidad, Colorado, as a water purification specialist, he had worked with arsenic and had died such a mysterious death, she apparently did nothing to try to dissuade Michael, and even encouraged him to put in for the same training in the army.

In fact, Michael did train to become a water purification specialist, and in his lab course, he did work with vials of arsenic, seemingly without untoward incidents. After he completed basic training, he was ordered to Fort Benning, Georgia, and on the way, stopped to visit his mother in Gulf Breeze, Florida.

It was during his time at home that he started to complain of prickling and tingling sensations in his hands and feet, but no one was unduly alarmed, and after a brief visit, he continued on his way to report for duty at Fort Benning. However, by then, his symptoms had worsened. He experienced nausea and vomiting, white lines appeared across all his fingernails, and he confronted a definite numbness in every extremity, sufficiently problematic that Michael checked himself in at the base hospital.

His condition continued to deteriorate, and his physicians, who were concerned about base metal poisoning, transferred him to the army's Walter Reed Hospital in Washington, where tests showed seven times the normal level of arsenic in his body. Not much could be done to reverse the devastating symptoms. The only recourse was to outfit him with full leg braces and a prosthetic device on his right hand, all of which combined to weigh about sixty pounds.

Michael had lost almost forty pounds of body weight; within six weeks his extremities atrophied enough that he could no longer walk or use his hands. Even after intense physical therapy, it became obvious he would never be able to be totally independent. He did learn to feed himself with his hand prosthesis, but he would always require the use of a wheelchair, a devastating future for any young man.

On May 12, the physicians sent him home to be cared for by his mother.

In all likelihood Judi had been formulating her plans, for just one day later, Michael was dead. Although her attempts to poison him had failed, there were other ways.

The day after he came home, Michael, his younger brother, James, and their mother went canoeing on the East River near Milton, Florida. The canoe was a two-seater, with one seat at the front, the other at the back, and a brace across the center. Judi and James had tied an aluminum lawn chair to the brace for Michael.

Sister Kimberly remained on shore to fish from the bank because of her severe allergy to the sun, while Judi and James paddled out into the river, with Michael fishing from the center of the canoe.

From that point on, what happened is murky. James and his mother told slightly different stories and slightly different versions every time they told them. But it seemed they were fishing close to the shore when either their fishing line became entangled in an overhead tree branch, or the bottom of their canoe hit a submerged log, or a snake dropped into the canoe, and in the resulting confusion they capsized. Whatever it was that happened, the canoe overturned, and despite the fact that doctors had stated it would be impossible for him to swim, Michael had not been strapped in and he was tossed into the water. Judi and James both tried to help him, but he was gone.

Their screams and shouts attracted the attention of a man who was fishing in the river downstream. The man, Ricky Hicks, hurriedly turned his boat around and upon reaching Judi and James, he helped them both into his boat. Judi told him there was another son with them, but when Hicks began to search the waters, she asked instead to be taken back upstream to call for help and wait for rescuers to arrive. Even though Hicks thought that minutes or even seconds might be crucial, she asked for and drank a can of his beer while she waited for the police and a diving team to come search for her son. In three hours, Michael was back. He was dead, but he was back.

Judi claimed to love her son and to be devastated by his death, but she recovered immediately, collected on his three insurance policies, and promptly opened a beauty salon in Gulf Breeze, named Fingers N Faces. This woman, who had over the years in various places made claim to being an LPN, an RN with PhDs in psychology and biochemistry, head nurse at West Florida Hospital, and even an MD, now bragged that she had a "string of degrees as long as my arm" and made "five hundred thousand dollars a year." With Lady Luck smiling on her, Judi wasted no time in moving on.

Not only did she move on to open her own business, but it was about then that she met John Wesley Gentry II at a nightclub. Gentry was a Pensacola businessman who owned a successful carpet and wallpaper business. At last, Judi embarked on a new romance that was much to her liking, one involving Caribbean cruises, expensive gifts, champagne, and fine dining. After six months, they moved in together, John, Judi, and Judi's teenagers, James and Kimberly.

In October 1982, the owners of Fingers N Faces and Gentry's Wallpaper Mill Outlet took out fifty-thousand-dollar life insurance policies on each other, but Gentry was unaware that on her own, Judi later increased the value of the one on him to five hundred thousand dollars and paid the increased premiums herself. Shortly after that, she convinced Gentry that it would be a good thing for him to begin taking vitamins, which she was only too happy to supply. Even when he became dizzy and nauseous, she assured him he needed to double the dose, and he trusted her. She was a nurse, after all.

On the evening of June 25, 1983, Judi had planned a party to honor one of her employees who was moving away. There would be about six other women who worked in the shop, plus their husbands or dates. She would necessarily stay a bit late at the shop to attend to some business, and Gentry agreed to greet and seat the guests for her at the Driftwood Restaurant, where the party was to be held. She would be driving her white Corvette and would get there as fast as she could, she said, and then she dropped a bomb.

She told him she had seen a doctor that morning and she was pregnant. It was a shock. They never planned for more family, and there were already two teenagers in the house. They would talk later, she said, hinting about a possible abortion. But in the next breath, she asked if maybe he would want to get some champagne on his way home for them to have a private celebration of sorts. He thought it was strange, but decided the decision should be hers.

Judi also specified that when he arrived at the restaurant, he should not park directly in front of the Driftwood, but should put his car down the street at the far end of the parking lot. That seemed somewhat peculiar, but not worth fussing about, even when he arrived at the restaurant and saw her Corvette parked in front of the Driftwood. Besides, Judi had a lot on her mind that day, so he did as she asked.

The party went well, so well that at about 10:30 the women wanted just a few more drinks together. Judi told Gentry to go on home ahead of her and she would be there shortly to share the bottle of champagne he was going to pick up.

He was thinking about where he should go to pick up a bottle of special champagne as he turned the key in the ignition. It was the last thing he knew before the bomb went off, propelling him back to Vietnam, a Marine on patrol. He smelled that acid smell, same as a land mine. He felt as if he was hurtling down a long tunnel. Then he felt a pain, sharp, in his neck. His hands were covered with blood when he put them on his neck. His shoes were blown off his feet. He pushed open the car door, struggling against the pain to get out of the car, and trying to remember something—anything. Did the car battery explode? He tried to walk, but collapsed on the sidewalk.

He saw Judi in the crowd that gathered as they were loading him into an ambulance. She was screaming, hysterical. It was the last thing he remembered.

Judi's latest victim, however, was her luckiest one. Gentry was rushed to the hospital, was treated in the ER, and survived.

An investigation started immediately. Among the incidents Gentry related as soon as he was able to talk was the information about feeling ill after taking the vitamins Judi had given him. Fortunately, he had a few of the capsules left that he had only pretended to take, and he turned them over to the police. An analysis showed there was paraformaldehyde in them, a poison having no recognized medical use. The investigation of the Black Widow, as the authorities were beginning to call her, proceeded in earnest.

Judi was arrested and charged with the attempted murder of John W. Gentry. Shortly thereafter, she was also indicted, arrested, and jailed for the murder of her son Michael.

Meanwhile, handwriting experts examined the insurance applications for the policies Judi had collected on, and they detected forgeries on those for Michael and for Bobby Joe Morris. The court ordered Morris's body exhumed; tests on his body revealed arsenic levels high enough to kill eleven people. A few days later, Goodyear's body was exhumed with the same results. The wheels of justice turned faster.

On March 31, 1984, Judi was found guilty of the murder of her son, Michael. She was sentenced to life imprisonment without parole for the first twenty-five years. Then on October 1984, it took the jury less than two hours to find her guilty of attempted murder in the case of John Gentry. Her sentence for the second murder was twelve years, to run consecutively with the life term for Michael's murder. Just one year later, she was judged guilty at the trial for the murder of her first husband, James Goodyear, and was sentenced to death by electrocution.

Judi spent the next thirteen years alone in her cell at Broward County Correctional Center at Pembroke Pines, where each inmate spends an average of twenty-three hours a day in a cell measuring six by nine feet, with no air-conditioning and three meals a day served through an opening in the cell door. Most of her time was consumed with crocheting blankets and baby clothes, which she gave to her daughter to sell. She read a great deal, wrote many letters, and never admitted her guilt. After denying the existence of God for most of her life, having angrily rejected a gold crucifix on a necklace from Gentry at one time, Judi claimed to have found Jesus on Death Row. She even led Bible studies for other inmates.

A stay of execution was granted while appeals were filed. The case dragged on until her last appeal was turned down in 1998, but authorities in Colorado made it known that they were ready to file murder charges for the death of Bobby Joe Morris.

On March 30, 1998, after a last meal of broccoli, asparagus, strawberries, and tea, a frail, trembling Judi was almost carried into the death chamber at Florida State Prison.

She did not look at the forty-six witnesses watching from behind a glass partition. She closed her eyes, and had no last words to say before 2,300 volts of electricity shot through her flinching body. Five minutes later, she was pronounced dead on the day that would have been her son Michael's thirty-seventh birthday.

The first female electrocuted in the state undeniably qualified to join the rest of the jerks in Florida history.

Bibliography

Dr. Weedon's Gruesome Surgery

Hartley, William and Ellen. *Osceola, The Unconquered Indian.* New York: Hawthorne Books, Inc., 1973.

Mahon, John K. *History of the Second Seminole War.* Gainesville, FL: University Press of Florida, 1967.

Ward, Mary McNeer. "The Disappearance of the Head of Osceola." *Florida Historical Quarterly,* Volume 33, No. 3–4, Jan./Apr. 1955.

Weisman, Brent Richards. *Unconquered People: Florida's Seminole & Miccosukee Indians.* Gainesville, FL: University Press of Florida, 1999.

Wickman, Patricia Riles. *Osceola's Legacy.* Tuscaloosa, AL: The University of Alabama, 2006.

Wickman, Dr. P. R. "Death of Osceola: Most Famous Indian of His Day." *The Seminole Tribune,* Vol. XX, No. 19, January 23, 1998.

John Wilkes Booth's Florida Conspirator

Kauffman, Michael W. *American Brutus.* New York: Random House, 2004.

Ownsbey, Betty J. *Alias "Paine": Lewis Thorton Powell, The Mystery Man of the Lincoln Conspiracy.* Jefferson, NC: McFarland & Company, 1993.

Prior, Leon O. "Lewis Payne, Pawn of John Wilkes Booth." *Florida Historical Quarterly,* Volume XLIII, No. 1, July 1964.

Robison, Jim. Articles, *Orlando Sentinel* staff, June 2, 1992; June 28, 1992; November 14, 1993; November 13, 1994; December 4, 1994; November 5, 1995; July 13, 2003.

Swanson, James L. *Manhunt.* New York: Harper Collins, 2006.

The Carpetbagger Governor

Current, Richard N. *Three Carpetbag Governors.* Baton Rouge, LA: Louisiana State University Press, 1967.

Parks, Arva Moore. "Miami in 1876." *Tequesta,* No. XXV, 1975, Miami, FL: Historical Museum of Southern Florida.

Tebeau, Charlton, W. and Wm. Marina. *A History of Florida,* 3rd edition. Coral Gables, FL, 1999.

Williamson, Edward C. "Florida's First Reconstruction Legislature." *Florida Historical Quarterly,* Vol. 32, Issue 01, July 1953.

Florida's Green Menace

Bair, Cinnamon. "Water Hyacinth Was a Disaster." *The Ledger,* Lakeland, FL, May 23, 2010.

Buker, George E. "Engineers vs. Florida's Green Menace." *Florida Historical Quarterly,* Vol. LX, No. 4, April 1982.

Pollack, Andrew W. "Environmental Protection Agency Denies an Environmental Group's Request to Ban a Widely Used Weed Killer." *New York Times,* April 10, 2012.

Tacio, Henrylito D. "Water Hyacinth Ecological Value, Environmental Impacts." *Gaia Discovery,* August 15, 2009.

The Burning of Styx

Beasley, Adam H. "Henry Flagler, His Town, and the Fire." *Miami Herald,* February 4, 2012.

Chandler, David Leon. *Henry Flagler, The Astonishing Life & Times of the Visionary Robber Baron Who Founded Florida.* New York: Macmillan Publishing Company, 1986.

Martin, Sidney Walter. *Flagler's Florida.* Athens, GA: The University Press of Georgia, 1949.

"An Important Real Estate Deal." *Palm Beach Daily News,* March 13, 1910.

Tuckwood, Jan, and Eliot Kleinberg. *Pioneers in Paradise.* Marietta, GA: Longstreet Press, 1994.

Booker T. Washington Gives a Speech

Norrell, Robert J. *Up from History.* Cambridge, MA: The Belknap Press/Harvard University Press, 2011.

Washington, Booker T. *Up from Slavery.* Secaucus, NJ: Carol Publishing Group, 1997.

White, Arthur O. "Booker T. Washington's Florida Incident, 1903–1904." *Florida Historical Quarterly,* Vol. 51, No. 3, January 1973.

———. "Race, Politics, and Education: The Sheats-Holloway Election Controversy, 1903–1904." *Florida Historical Quarterly,* Vol. LIII, No. 3, January 1975.

Guy Bradley's Killer

Davis, Jack E., and Raymond Arsenault. *Paradise Lost?* Gainesville, FL: University Press of Florida, 2005.

McIver, Stuart. *Death in the Everglades.* Gainesville, FL: University Press of Florida, 2003.

"Florida Fisherman Who Shot Game Warden Says It Was Done in Self-Defense." *New York Times,* June 8, 1909.

Pierce, Charles William. "The Cruise of the *Bonton.*" *Tequesta,* 1962.

Edgar J. Watson: Killing Machine

Davis, Jack E. "From 'Nuisance' to Treasure." *FORUM: The Magazine of the Florida Humanities Council,* Summer 2002.

"The Killing of Mr. Watson." *Coastal Breeze News,* October 21, 2010.

Author's telephone conversation with historian Alvin Lederer, July 27, 2012.

McIver, Stuart. *True Tales of the Everglades.* Miami, FL: Florida Flair Books, 1989.

Historic Peace River Valley Florida. *Edgar J. Watson's Graveyard of Horror—Chokoloskee, Florida.* April 15, 2011.

Storter, Rob. *Crackers in the Glade, Life and Times in the Old Everglades.* Athens, GA: University of Georgia Press, 2000.

Tebeau, Charlton. *Story of Chokoloskee Bay Country.* Coral Gables, FL: University of Miami Press, 1955.

The Divisive Governor Catts

Chalmers, David. "The Ku Klux Klan in the Sunshine State: the 1920s." *Florida Historical Quarterly,* Vol. 42, No. 3, January 1964.

Doherty, Jr., Herbert J. "Florida and the Presidential Election of 1928." *Florida Historical Quarterly,* Vol. XXVI, No. 2, October 1947.

Flynt, Wayne. *Cracker Messiah.* Baton Rouge, LA: Louisiana State University Press, 1977.

———. "William V. Knott and the Gubernatorial Campaign of 1916." *Florida Historical Quarterly,* Vol. LI, No. 4, April 1973.

Jennings, Warren A. "Sidney Catts and the Democratic Primary of 1920." *Florida Historical Quarterly,* Vol. 39, Issue 3, January 1961.

Kerber, Stephen. "Park Trammell and the Florida Democratic Senatorial Primary of 1916." *Florida Historical Quarterly,* Vol. LVIII, No. 3, January 1980.

Page, David. "Bishop Michael J. Curley and Anti-Catholic Nativism in Florida." *Florida Historical Quarterly,* Vol. XLV, No. 2, October 1966.

Tuckwood, Jan, and Eliot Kleinberg. *Pioneers in Paradise.* Athens, GA: Longstreet Press, 1994.

III Years of Child Cruelty

Carper, N. Gordon. "Martin Tabert, Martyr of an Era." *Florida Historical Quarterly,* Vol. 52, Issue 2, October 1973.

Fisher, Robin Gaby, with Michael O'McCarthy and Robert W. Straley. *The Boys of the Dark,* New York: St. Martin's Press, 2010.

Miller, Carol Marbin. "Feds Condemn Conditions at Florida Youth Prisons." *Miami Herald,* December 2, 2011.

Montgomery, Ben, and Waveney Ann Moore. "For Their Own Good: a St. Petersburg Times Special Report on Child Abuse at the Florida School for Boys." *St. Petersburg Times,* April 17, 2009.

———. "Infamous School for Boys Will Shed the Dozier Name." *St. Petersburg Times,* May 12, 2010.

Ben Hecht Buries a Treasure

Clark, James C. *200 Quick Looks at Florida History.* Sarasota, FL: Pineapple Press, Inc., 2000.

Hecht, Ben. *A Child of the Century.* Plume New York: 1954.

McAdams, Wm. *Ben Hecht, a Biography.* New York: Charles Scribner's Sons, 1990.

Weiss, Murray, and Bill Hoffman. *Palm Beach Babylon.* New York: Carol Publishing Group, 1992.

Pepper, Ball, and Gorgeous George

Bousquet, Steve. "Florida Politics Churns Mud Faster Than a Swamp Buggy in the Glades." *Tampa Bay Times,* October 9, 2010.

Clark, James C. "Claude Pepper and the Seeds of His 1950 Defeat: 1944–1948." *Florida Historical Quarterly,* Vol. 74, No. 1, Summer 1995.

Danese, Tracy E. *Claude Pepper and Ed Ball.* Gainesville, FL: University Press of Florida, 2000.

Nohlgren, Stephen. "A Born Winner, If Not a Native Floridian." *St. Petersburg Times,* November 29, 2003.

Pepper, Denson Claude, with Hays Gorey. *Pepper, Eyewitness to a Century.* G.K. Holt, & Co., Boston, MA: 1987.

The Trial of Marjorie Kinnan Rawlings

Acton, Patricia Nassif. *Invasion of Privacy: The Cross Creek Trial of Marjorie Kinnan Rawlings.* Gainesville, FL: University Press of Florida, 1988.

Bigelow, Gordon, and Laura V. Monit, eds. *Selected Letters of Marjorie Kinnan Rawlings.* Gainesville, FL: University Press of Florida, 1982.

Davis, Robert Curtis, VP Marjorie Kinnan Rawlings Society. *My Friend Dessie.* Indialantic, FL: Eulogy, April 28, 2002.

Glisson, J. T. *The Creek.* Gainesville, FL: University Press of Florida, 1993.

Parker, Idella, with Bud and Liz Crussell. *Idella Parker: From Reddick to Cross Creek.* Gainesville, FL: University Press of Florida, 1999.

Rawlings, Marjorie Kinnan. *Cross Creek.* New York: Charles Scribner's Sons, 1942.

Silverthorne, Elizabeth. *Marjorie Kinnan Rawlings, Sojourner at Cross Creek.* Woodstock, NY: The Overlook Press, 1988.

Sheriff McCall's Brutal Reign

Hill, John. "A Southern Sheriff's Law and Order." *St. Petersburg Times,* November 28, 1999.

King, Gilbert. *Devil in the Grove.* New York: Harper Collins, 2012.

Lawson, Steven F., David R. Colburn, and Darryl Paulson. "Groveland: Florida's Little Scotsboro." *Florida Historical Quarterly,* Vol. 65, No. 2, July 1986.

"National Affairs: The Sheriff Shoots." *Time,* November 19, 1951.

Newton, Michael. *The Invisible Empire.* Gainesville, FL: University Press of Florida, 2001.

"Florida: Murmur in the Streets." *Time,* August 1, 1949.

Trippett, Frank. "High and Mighty Sheriff." *LIFE Magazine,* November 17, 1972.

KKK: Organized Jerks

D'Orso, Michael. *Like Judgment Day.* New York: G. P. Putman's Sons, 1996.

Green, Ben. *Before His Time.* Gainesville, FL: University Press of Florida, 1999.

Newton, Michael. *The Invisible Empire.* Gainesville, FL: University Press of Florida, 2001.

"Suspects Named in Moore's Murder" *AGNews,* Attorney General Consumer Bulletin, August 24, 2006.

Taylor, Robert A. *Florida, An Illustrated History.* New York: Hippocrene Books, Inc., 2005.

Wade, Wyn Craig. *The Firey Cross.* New York: Simon & Schuster, 1998.

McCarthyism Invades Florida

Bertwell, Dan. "'A Veritable Refuge for Practicing Homosexuals': The Johns Committee and the University of South Florida." *The Florida Historical Quarterly,* Vol. 83, No. 4, Summer 2005.

"Florida Examines Era of Suspicion." *New York Times,* July 4, 1993.

Graves, Karen L. *And They Were Wonderful Teachers: Florida's Purge of Gay and Lesbian Teachers.* Urbana, IL: University of Illinois Press, 2010.

Howard, John. *Carryin' On in the Lesbian and Gay South.* New York: New York University Press, 1997.

Huse, Andrew. "USF History 101—The Witch Hunt Comes to USF." *The Oracle,* University of South Florida, September 23, 2003.

Newman, Jessica. "Behind Closed Doors: The Dark Legacy of the Johns Committee." The *Gainesville Iguana,* November 5, 2011.

Schnur, James A. *Cold Warriors in the Hot Sunshine: USF and the Johns Committee.* Masters' thesis, University of South Florida, 1985.

Schrecker, Ellen. *The Age of McCarthyism: A Brief History with Documents.* New York: St. Martin's Press, 1994.

Justice for Adam

Kruse, Michael. "Safety and Fear Make up Adam Walsh's Legacy." *Tampa Bay Times,* December 22, 2008.

Palmer, Rhett. "Rhett's Page 2 Interview with John Walsh." *Vero's Voice,* pp.1–3, Issue 13.

Standiford, Les, with Det. Sgt. Joe Matthews. *Bringing Adam Home.* New York: Ecco, Imprint of Harper Collins, 2011.

Walsh, John, with Susan Schindehette. *Tears of Rage.* New York: Pocketbooks, Div. of Simon & Schuster, 1997.

Even Heroes Can Be Jerks

Ackman, Martha. *The Mercury Thirteen*. New York: Random House, 2003.

Cochran, Jacqueline, and Maryann Bucknum Brinley. *Jackie Cochran, the Autobiography of the Greatest Woman Pilot in Aviation History* New York: Bantam Books, Inc., 1987.

Madrigal, Alexis. "The Women Who Would Have Been Sally Ride." *The Atlantic,* July 24, 2012.

Rich, Doris. *Jackie Cochran, Pilot in the Fastest Lane*. Gainesville, FL: University Press of Florida, 2007.

Steadman, Bernice Trimble. *Tethered Mercury*. Traverse City, MI: Aviation Press, 2001.

Queen of Florida Jerks

Anderson, Chris, and Sharon McGehee. *Bodies of Evidence*. New York: Carol Publishing Group, 1991.

"Death Row from the inside." *Tampa Bay Times,* May 24, 2004.

"Florida Puts to Death First Woman in 150 Years." *New York Times,* March 31, 1998.

Roy, Roger. "Woman Denies Poisoning Husband." *Orlando Sentinel,* October 30, 1985.

Index

About the Author

E. Lynne Wright is the author of *It Happened in Florida, More than Petticoats: Remarkable Florida Women, Disasters and Heroic Rescues of Florida: True Stories of Tragedy and Survival, Florida: Mapping the Sunshine State through History* (with Vincent Virga), and *Myths and Mysteries of Florida,* all published by Globe Pequot Press. Her short stories, nonfiction articles, essays, and book reviews have appeared in the *Cleveland Plain Dealer, Hartford Courant, Woman's Day,* and many anthologies and literary magazines. She lives in Vero Beach, Florida.